COMBO SPLIT 2A

Catherine Frazier | Richard Frazier

Jennifer Wilkin | Carmella Lieske

HEINLE
CENGAGE Learning

Australia • Brazil • Japan • Korea • Mexico • Singapore • Spain • United Kingdom • United States

HEINLE
CENGAGE Learning™

Time Zones Combo Split 2A
Catherine Frazier
Richard Frazier
Jennifer Wilkin
Carmella Lieske

Publisher: Andrew Robinson

Executive Editor: Sean Bermingham

Senior Development Editors: Ian Purdon,
    Derek Mackrell

Assistant Editor: Claire Tan

Contributing Editor: Eunice Yeates

National Geographic Editorial Coordinator:
    Leila Hishmeh

Senior Technology Development Manager:
    Debie Mirtle

Technology Project Manager: Pam Prater

Director of Global Marketing: Ian Martin

Senior Product Marketing Manager:
    Katie Kelley

Assistant Marketing Manager: Jide Iruka

Content Project Manager: Tan Jin Hock

Senior Print Buyer: Mary Beth Hennebury

Compositor: Page 2, LLC.

Cover/Text Designer: Page 2, LLC.

Cover Art Illustrations: Gaim Creative Studio
    and Imaginary FS Pte. Ltd.
Cover Photos: (from top left) David Doubilet/
    National Geographic Image Collection; NASA/
    National Geographic Image Collection; Greg
    Girard/National Geographic Image Collection;
    Stephen Alvarez/National Geographic
    Image Collection; Yongkang Zheng,
    ChinaPhoto-World.com; Gordon Wiltsie/
    National Geographic Image Collection; Ralph
    Lee Hopkins/National Geographic Image
    Collection; JIS/Shutterstock

Combo Split 2A ISBN-13: 978-1-4240-6121-1

Combo Split 2A ISBN-10: 1-4240-6121-0

Combo Split 2A + Student Multi-ROM ISBN-13: 978-1-4240-6447-2

Combo Split 2A + Student Multi-ROM ISBN-10: 1-4240-6447-3

Heinle
20 Channel Center Street
Boston, MA 02210
USA

Cengage Learning is a leading provider of customized learning solutions with office locations around the globe, including Singapore, the United Kingdom, Australia, Mexico, Brazil, and Japan. Locate your local office at:
international.cengage.com/region

Cengage Learning products are represented in Canada by Nelson Education, Ltd.

Visit Heinle online at **elt.heinle.com**

Visit our corporate website at **www.cengage.com**

Printed in Canada
2 3 4 5 6 7 — 13 12 11 10

Table of Contents

The page numbers in the Combo Split match the page numbers in the full Student Book and Workbook. This helps classes in which both split and full editions are used. The following pages therefore do not appear in this book: Student Book 60–117, 119–120, 126–129, 134–135; Workbook 30–57, 60–61.

Acknowledgments

The authors and publisher would like to thank the following individuals who offered many helpful insights, ideas, and suggestions during the development of **Time Zones**.

Richard Ascough, Wayo Women's University, Chiba; **Simone Ashton**, Britanic Madalena, Recife; **Keith Astle**, Britanic Piedade, Jaboatão dos Guararapes; **João Alfredo Bergmann**, Instituto Cultural Brasileiro Norte-Americano, Porto Alegre; **Jeane Blume Cortezia**, Unisinos, Porto Alegre; **Lilian Bluvol Vaisman**, IBEU, Rio de Janeiro; **Adriane Caldas**, Colégio Anchieta, Porto Alegre; **Dulce Capiberibe**, Britanic Setúbal, Recife; **Flávia Carneiro**, ABA, Recife; **Mônica Carvalho**, ABA, Recife; **Shu-Yi Chang**, Ming Dao High School, Taichung; **Corina C. Machado Corrêa**, Alumni, São Paulo; **Samara Camilo Tomé Costa**, IBEU, Rio de Janeiro; **Silvia Regina D'Andrea**, União Cultural, São Paulo; **Gislaine Deckmann**, Unisinos, Porto Alegre; **José Olavo de Amorim**, Colégio Bandeirantes, São Paulo; **Stewart Dorward**, Shumei Junior and Senior High School, Saitama; **Andrei dos Santos Cunha**, Unisinos, Porto Alegre; **Kirvin Andrew Dyer**, Yan Ping High School, Taipei; **Sylvia Formoso**, Colégio Anchieta, Porto Alegre; **Allynne Fraemam**, ABA, Recife; Carmen Gehrke, Quatrum, Porto Alegre; **Elizabeth Gonçalves**, ICBEU, Rio de Janeiro; **Carlos Olavo Queiroz Guimarães**, IBEU, Rio de Janeiro; **Rosana Gusmão**, Unisinos, Porto Alegre; **Rui-Hua Hsu**, Chi Yong High School, Taichung; **Ken Hsi Ip**, Mejiro Kenshin Junior and Senior High School, Tokyo; **Thays Ladosky**, DAMAS, Recife; **Inês Greve Milke**, Instituto Cultural Brasileiro Norte-Americano, Porto Alegre; **Brigitte Mund**, Unisinos, Porto Alegre; **Andrew O'Brien**, Second Kyoritsu Girls Junior and Senior High School, Tokyo; **Matthew Gerard O'Conner**, Britanic Setúbal, Recife; **Atsuko Okada**, Shinagawa Joshi Gakuin Junior and Senior High School, Tokyo; **Simone Raupp**, Colégio Anchieta, Porto Alegre; **Jonathan Reinaux**, ABA, Recife; **Viviane Remígio**, Britanic Setúbal, Recife; **Rodrigo Rezende**, Seven, São Paulo; **Ruth Salomon-Barkemeyer**, Unilínguas Sao Leopoldo; **Carlos Santanna**, IEBEU, Rio de Janeiro; **Kate Sato**, Kitopia English School, Sapporo; **Daniel Stewart**, Kaisei Junior and Senior High School, Tokyo; **Ludwig Tan**, National Institute of Education, Singapore; **Tamami Wada**, Nanzan University, Aichi; **Philip Woodall**, Aoyama Gakuin High School, Tokyo; **Akira Yasuhara**, Rikkyo Ikebukuro Junior and Senior High School, Tokyo; **Sheila Yu**, Shin Min High School, Taichung

Thanks are due to **Milada Broukal**, **Janet Gokay**, **Paul MacIntyre**, and **Eunice Yeates** for their work in the development and editing of the series.

Additional thanks to **Diana Jaksic**, **Jim McClelland**, **Jim Burch**, and **Todd Hermann** at the National Geographic Society.

Welcome to

Time Zones !

In this series, you will learn to communicate in English with the help of our four young reporters. They will take you on a journey around the world and help you explore, discover, and learn!

EXPLORE

You will explore amazing places and fascinating cultures with National Geographic and our team of young global reporters.

DISCOVER

You will discover the exciting worlds of science, technology, nature, history, geography, and culture.

LEARN

You will learn how to use English to communicate effectively in the real world.

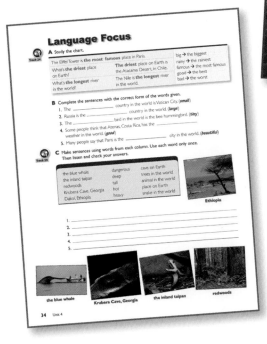

Now you're ready to take a journey through

Time Zones !

Scope and Sequence

Unit	Functions	Grammar
1 What do you like to do?	Talking about schedules and activities Talking about frequency **Real English:** *That's OK.* (changing the subject)	*like to* + verb Wh- question: *How often* Simple present
2 What does she look like?	Describing someone's appearance Describing emotions **Real English:** *Sorry.* (apologizing)	*look like* Adjectival order
3 How do you get to the park?	Asking for and giving directions Asking about transportation **Real English:** *right* (emphasizing exact place)	Imperatives (Directions) Prepositions of location

World Explorer New York City

Unit	Functions	Grammar
4 What's the coldest place on Earth?	Comparing things **Real English:** *Just a minute . . .* (delaying)	Regular and irregular superlative adjectives
5 Are cats *cuter* than dogs?	Comparing things **Real English:** *A spider?* (repeating to clarify)	Regular and irregular comparative adjectives *(not) as . . . as*
6 How was your trip?	Talking about past events Expressing agreement & disagreement **Real English:** *so* (emphasizing)	Simple past with regular and irregular verbs

World Explorer Antarctica

Vocabulary	Pronunciation	Reading	Writing
Hobbies and interests Time expressions	Reduction: *to*	Capoeira: The Fighting Dance	E-mail
Physical appearance Emotions	Blends: *bl, br, gl, gr*	Changing Faces	Short essay
Places around town Modes of transportation	*O* sounds	Visit Xi'an!	Tour guide
Continents Places in nature Large numbers	Sentence stress	Extreme Amazon	Travel poster
Animal characteristics Animals Body parts Emotions	Reduction: *than*	Working Dogs	Blog
Verb phrases Distance and height measurements	Regular past tense verb ending: *-ed* sounds	Around and Over the World	Blog

Unit 1

▶ Talk about your hobbies and interests ☐

▶ Describe your schedule ☐

Unit 2

▶ Describe how people look ☐

▶ Learn about masks ☐

2

People and Places

World Explorer
► Review the language from Units 1 to 3 ▪
► Learn about New York City ▪

Unit 3
► Ask for and give directions ▪
► Talk about places around town ▪

3

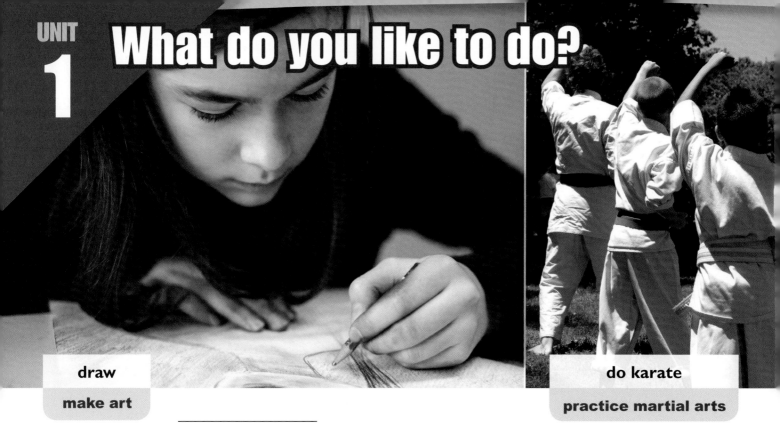

UNIT 1 What do you like to do?

draw

make art

_____

do karate

practice martial arts

_____

Preview

Track 1

A Some students are talking about their hobbies.
Listen and write their names under the pictures.

~~Amy~~   Pablo   Daniel   Matt   Sarah

Track 1

B Listen again. What do the students like to do? Complete the chart.

action figures   piano   volleyball   comic books
ice hockey   animals   karate   ~~guitar~~

Make art	Practice martial arts	Collect things	Play sports	Play an instrument
				guitar

C Take turns asking and answering questions with a partner.

A: Do you like to play sports?   A: What sports do you play?

B: Yes, I do.   B: I play tennis.

collect action figures

collect things

play volleyball

play sports

play the guitar

play an instrument

_____   _____   _____ *Amy* _____

Conversation

Track 2

A Listen to the conversation. Then listen again and repeat.

B Practice the conversation with a partner. Replace the words in **blue**.

Real English

That's OK.

1

What do you like to do after school, Stig?

I like to **play ice hockey**.

play volleyball
draw

2 How about you, Maya?

Well, I like to **play the guitar**. Hey, I can **play** for you!

play music / sing
play the piano / play

What's your favorite song? I can sing it for you.

3

Uh, Maya . . . what else do you like to do?

play the piano
dance

Well, I like to **sing**.

4

play a game
watch TV

That's OK, Maya. Let's **watch a movie!**

What do you like to do?   5

Language Focus

A Study the chart.

What **do** you **like to do** on weekdays / on weekends?	I **like to play** sports.	
Do you **like to play** tennis?	Yes, I **do**. / No, I **don't**.	I time = once 2 times = twice
What sports **do** you **play**? How often **does** he **play**? When **do** they **play**?	I **play** soccer and volleyball. He **plays three times a week**. They **play before / after** school.	

B Complete the questions. Then match each question to the correct answer.

1. What do you like _____*to do*_____ after school? ____*b*____

2. How often _____ they _____ tennis? _____

3. What sports _____ he _____? _____

4. Do you like _____ volleyball? _____

5. How often _____ you _____ the guitar? _____

6. When _____ she _____ karate? _____

a. They play twice a week.   d. He plays soccer.

b. I like to play games and read.   e. I play every day.

c. She does it after school.   f. No, I don't.

C Look at Nadine's schedule below and complete the conversation. Listen and check your answers. Then practice with a partner.

Nadine's Schedule

Monday	Tuesday	Wednesday	Thursday	Friday	Saturday	Sunday
			soccer			
SCHOOL 8:00–3:00					karate	
volleyball	guitar	volleyball	guitar	volleyball		

Ming: Nadine, what do you do (1) _____ school?

Nadine: Well, I play volleyball and I go to guitar class.

Ming: Really? (2) _____ do you play volleyball?

Nadine: I play (3) _____.

Ming: Do you do anything (4) _____ school
          (5) _____ weekdays?

Nadine: Yeah, I play soccer (6) _____ a week, on Thursdays.

Ming: What do you like to do (7) _____ Saturdays?

Nadine: Well, I do karate (8) _____. On Sundays, I do homework.

Pronunciation

A Listen to the sentences. Then listen again and repeat.

Reduction: to

1. What do you like to do?   I like to play volleyball.
2. Does she like to make art?   No, she doesn't.

B Listen to the sentences and fill in the blanks.

1. What do _____ do?
2. _____ do karate.
3. Do _____ play games?
4. _____ eat Korean food.
5. Does _____ play an instrument?
6. What TV shows do _____ watch?

C Take turns reading the sentences in B with a partner.

Do you **know** **?**

How many players are there on a volleyball team?
a. 2
b. 6
c. 11

Communication

Play bingo in small groups. Take turns asking a question about hobbies and interests. The other students answer and place a marker on the square that is true for them. The first student to complete a row wins.

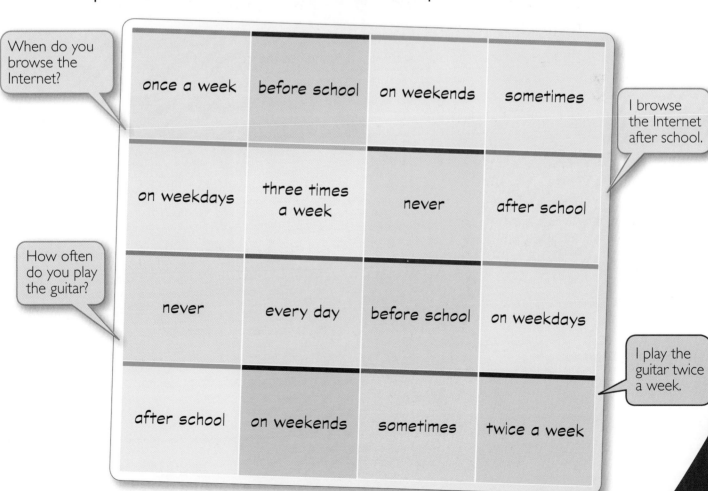

When do you browse the Internet?

I browse the Internet after school.

How often do you play the guitar?

I play the guitar twice a week.

once a week	before school	on weekends	sometimes
on weekdays	three times a week	never	after school
never	every day	before school	on weekdays
after school	on weekends	sometimes	twice a week

Reading

A Look at the title and the pictures. Who are these people? What are they doing? Tell a partner.

B Read the article and check your answers to A.

C Answer the questions on page 10.

Capoeira fighters make a large circle and dance.

Salvador, Brazil

Capoeira: The Fighting Dance

1 In a lot of places around the world, poor children live on the streets. These street children do not have homes or parents. They do not go to school and do not have hobbies. Their lives are very hard.

In Salvador, Brazil, a special group called the Axe Project helps street children. It finds
5 homes for the children and helps them go to school and study. It also teaches them capoeira.

Capoeira is a martial art, a game, and a dance. People make a large circle, sing, and play instruments. They sing sad songs and songs about life. Inside the circle, two people fight and dance. Like in karate and other martial arts, capoeira fighters wear white clothes.

10 Milton dos Santos, a 15-year-old boy, is learning capoeira. He loves it. He likes to dance and fight. This martial art teaches Milton self-respect and how to respect other people. Capoeira helps street children make new lives.

9

Comprehension

A Answer the questions about *Capoeira: The Fighting Dance.* Circle the correct answers.

1. Who does the Axe Project NOT help?

   a. teenagers   **b.** poor children   **c.** parents

2. What does "it" mean in line 5?

   a. the group   **b.** the school   **c.** the children

3. The people _____ inside the circle.

   a. sing   **b.** fight   **c.** play instruments

4. Capoeira fighters wear _____.

   a. karate clothes   **b.** sandals   **c.** white clothes

5. What does Milton dos Santos like to do?

   a. sing   **b.** dance   **c.** play instruments

Do you **know**?

Taekwondo is a martial art from _____.

a. Brazil
b. Korea
c. Japan

B Use the words below to complete the text.

helps teenagers	sing songs	have hobbies
wear white clothes	live on the streets	around the world

A lot of poor children _____ have hard lives.

They _____ because they don't have parents or homes.

They don't _____, like art, music, or collecting comic books.

In Salvador, Brazil, a group _____ study and find homes. The group teaches them capoeira, too.

Capoeira is a martial art. People _____ and make a circle.

They play music and _____ about life. People inside the circle fight and dance.

Writing

Read the e-mail. Then write a reply to a new e-pal about your hobbies and interests.

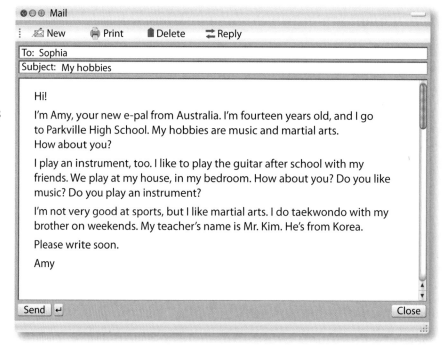

⊗⊖⊕ Mail

✉ New   🖨 Print   🗑 Delete   ⇄ Reply

To: Sophia

Subject: My hobbies

Hi!

I'm Amy, your new e-pal from Australia. I'm fourteen years old, and I go to Parkville High School. My hobbies are music and martial arts. How about you?

I play an instrument, too. I like to play the guitar after school with my friends. We play at my house, in my bedroom. How about you? Do you like music? Do you play an instrument?

I'm not very good at sports, but I like martial arts. I do taekwondo with my brother on weekends. My teacher's name is Mr. Kim. He's from Korea.

Please write soon.

Amy

Send ↵   Close

The Real World

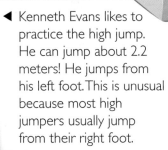

What can these kids do?

According to one polling company, 63 percent of Americans are sports fans, and 37 percent of Americans are not. Also, 41 percent of Americans like to watch football, 10 percent like to watch baseball, and 9 percent like to watch basketball. These are the number one sports in the United States.

◀ Kenneth Evans likes to practice the high jump. He can jump about 2.2 meters! He jumps from his left foot. This is unusual because most high jumpers usually jump from their right foot.

◀ Teenagers like to watch movies, but this teenager likes to make them! Patricio Lawson has a movie company. He makes cartoons.

A Work in small groups and prepare a poll. Interview the students in your group and make charts to show your results. Look at the examples.

1 Are you a sports fan?
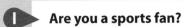

3 Do you like to play sports or watch them?

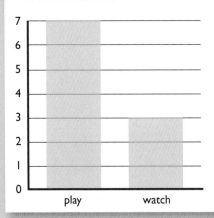

Idiom

"He has two left feet" means

_____.

a. he can run
b. he likes to fight
c. he can't dance

2 What's your favorite sport?
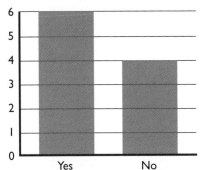

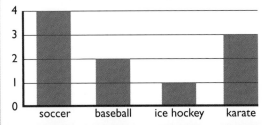

B Compare your group's results with other groups' results.

How many people are sports fans?

UNIT 2
What does she look like?

brown
eyes

short red
hair

brown
eyes

straight
black hair

_____

_____

Preview

Track 8

A What do these students look like? Listen and circle the correct words.

1. Jenny has (*curly* / *straight*) hair and (*blue* / *brown*) eyes.
2. Erin has (*long* / *short*) hair and (*green* / *blue*) eyes.
3. Max has (*spiky* / *short*) hair and (*brown* / *green*) eyes.
4. Josh has (*spiky* / *curly*) hair and (*green* / *blue*) eyes.
5. Tim has (*straight* / *curly*) hair and (*brown* / *blue*) eyes.

Track 8

B Label the pictures with each person's name. Listen again and check your answers.

C Take turns asking a partner questions about the pictures.

A: What color are her eyes?

B: They're green.

A: Does she have short hair?

B: No, it's long.

green eyes

spiky brown hair

curly brown hair

blue eyes

long blond hair

brown eyes

Conversation

Track 9

A Listen to the conversation. Then listen again and repeat.

B Practice the conversation with a partner. Replace the words in **blue**.

Real English

Sorry.

1 Hey, Ming, I'm at the **soccer** game. Where are you?

Sorry, I'm late. I'm on the train.

hockey
rugby

2 Do you see my friend Emily?

What does she look like?

She has **short blond** hair and **blue** eyes.

long brown / brown
spiky red / brown

3 What's she wearing?

She's wearing a **red** T-shirt.

blue
green

Oh, yes. I see her. She's over there.

4 Excuse me, are you . . . ? **Stig**!

Hi, Nadine!

Maya
Max

What does she look like?   13

Language Focus

A Study the chart.

What **does** he **look like**?	He's **tall** and he **has short curly blond** hair.
What **do** you **look like**?	I'm **short** and I **have long straight red** hair. I **have** braces and I **wear** glasses. I'm **medium height** and I **have** freckles.

B Look at the pictures. What do they look like? Complete the sentences.

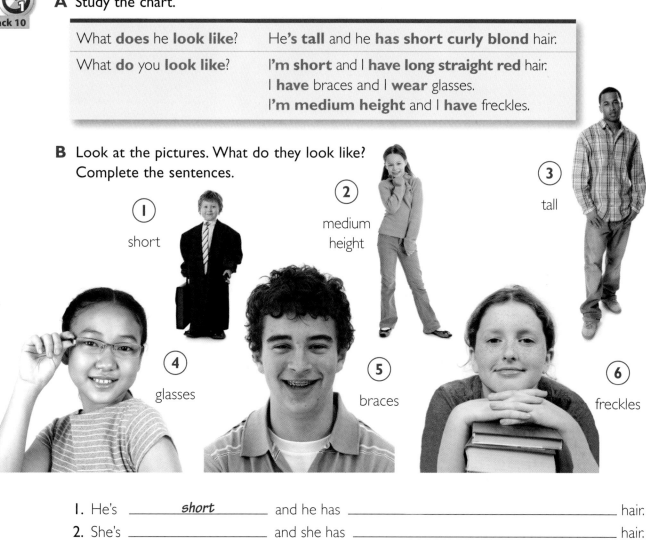

① short

② medium height

③ tall

④ glasses

⑤ braces

⑥ freckles

1. He's _____*short*_____ and he has _____ hair.
2. She's _____ and she has _____ hair.
3. He's _____ and _____.
4. She wears _____ and she has _____.
5. He has _____.
6. She _____.

C Unscramble the sentences. Listen and check your answers. Then practice with a partner.

1. A: Hey, there's a new boy in class.
   B: he / like / What / look / does _____?
   A: has / hair / He / and / blond / 's / tall / he _____
   _____.

2. A: Do you see my sisters?
   B: look / What / do / like / they _____?
   A: short / they / wear / hair / They / glasses / black / and / have _____
   _____.

14   Unit 2

Pronunciation

Track 12

A Listen to the words. Then listen again and repeat.

Blends: *bl, br, gl, gr*

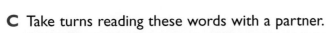

1. blue   3. glasses
2. brown   4. gray

Track 13

B Listen to the words. Circle the sound you hear.

1. bl / br / gl / gr   5. bl / br / gl / gr
2. bl / br / gl / gr   6. bl / br / gl / gr
3. bl / br / gl / gr   7. bl / br / gl / gr
4. bl / br / gl / gr   8. bl / br / gl / gr

Do you know ?

Which country has the highest percentage of redheads?
a. Scotland
b. France
c. Russia

C Take turns reading these words with a partner.

blond	bread	great	black
grapes	glasses	grandmother	brother

Communication

A Think of some famous people or cartoon characters. What do they look like?
Complete the chart.

Person	Hair	Eyes	Body	More information
Shrek	no hair	brown	big, tall	He's green.

B Work with a partner. Describe someone from your list. Your partner guesses who it is.
Take turns.

What does your person look like?

Is it Shrek?

Well, he doesn't have hair. He's big and tall. He has brown eyes. He's green, too!

Yes!

Reading

A Look at the title and the pictures.
What do you think the article is about?

   a. the history of masks

   b. masks in Bali, Indonesia

   c. how to make masks

B Read the article and check your answer to A.

C Answer the questions on page 18.

Ronald Naversen's mask collection

mask

nose

teeth

mouth

ears

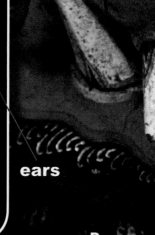

a Barong costume and mask from Bali

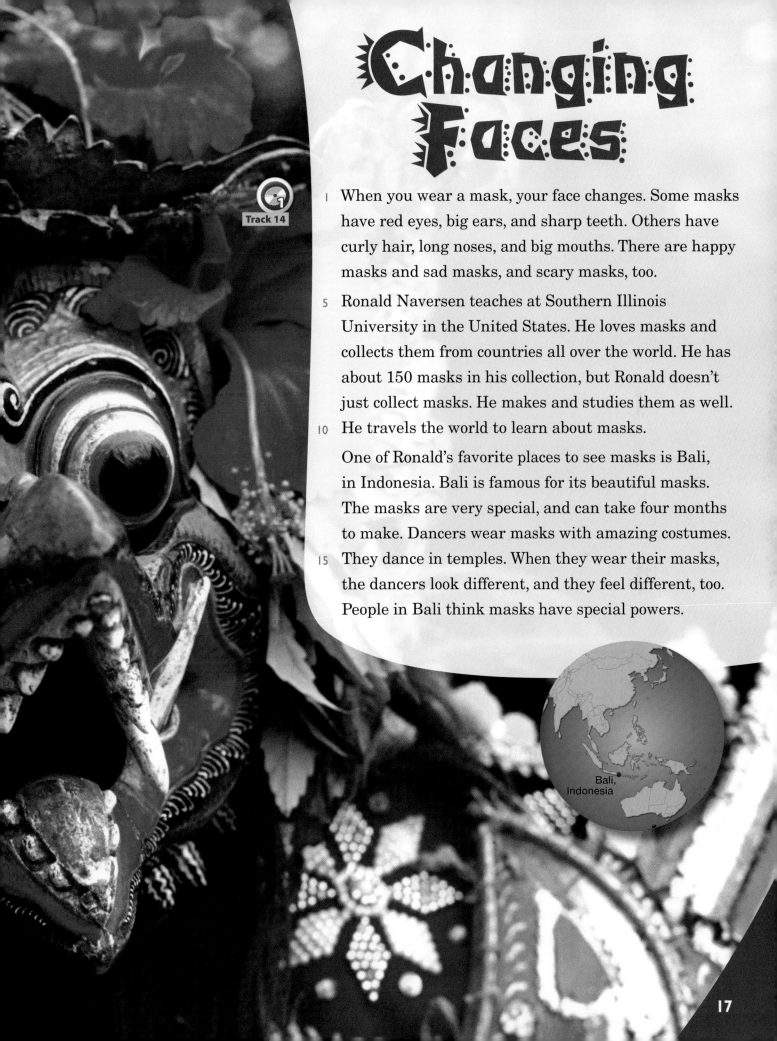

Changing Faces

Track 14

1 When you wear a mask, your face changes. Some masks have red eyes, big ears, and sharp teeth. Others have curly hair, long noses, and big mouths. There are happy masks and sad masks, and scary masks, too.

5 Ronald Naversen teaches at Southern Illinois University in the United States. He loves masks and collects them from countries all over the world. He has about 150 masks in his collection, but Ronald doesn't just collect masks. He makes and studies them as well.

10 He travels the world to learn about masks.

One of Ronald's favorite places to see masks is Bali, in Indonesia. Bali is famous for its beautiful masks. The masks are very special, and can take four months to make. Dancers wear masks with amazing costumes.

15 They dance in temples. When they wear their masks, the dancers look different, and they feel different, too. People in Bali think masks have special powers.

Bali,
Indonesia

Comprehension

A Answer the questions about *Changing Faces*.

1. What does "others" mean in line 2?

    a. eyes   **b.** teeth   **c.** masks

2. What is Ronald Naversen's job?

    a. he is a teacher   **b.** he travels   **c.** he makes masks

3. How many masks does Ronald Naversen have?

    a. 8   **b.** 40   **c.** 150

4. Which statement about masks in Bali is true?

    a. They only take a short time to make.

    b. People don't think they are beautiful.

    c. Some people think they have special powers.

5. What do we NOT find out from the article?

    a. what some masks look like

    b. how much the masks cost

    c. where Ronald works

Do you **know?**

When do kids in the United States wear masks and celebrate Halloween?
a. September
b. October
c. November

B Look at the masks from Ronald Naversen's collection on page 16. Match the masks to the descriptions. Then choose another mask and describe it to a partner. Can your partner guess which one it is?

a. _____ This mask has large eyes, big ears, and a red face.

b. _____ This mask has large eyes, a red mouth, and a white face.

c. _____ This mask has spiky gray hair. It's a monkey mask.

Writing

A Make a word web to describe the way you look. Then write a paragraph on a piece of paper about yourself. Don't write your name!

height   hair

eyes   What I look like

B Get into groups and shuffle the paragraphs. Then read them aloud. Can you guess your classmates from their descriptions?

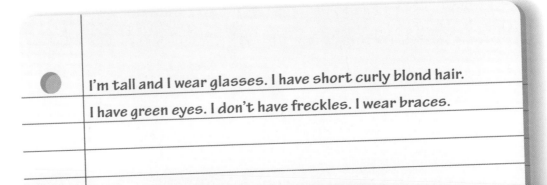

I'm tall and I wear glasses. I have short curly blond hair.

I have green eyes. I don't have freckles. I wear braces.

The Real World

What does your face say?

Can you guess how people feel when you look at their faces? Each feeling has its own facial expression, or the way someone's face looks. For example, a smile usually means someone is happy. A scientist named Paul Ekman made a list of feelings. There are 3,000 different facial expressions on his list!

How do these people feel? Write the words below each picture.

| afraid | angry | happy | sad | surprised |

1. _____

2. _____

3. _____

Idiom

"Keep a straight face" means don't
_____.
a. talk
b. be sad
c. laugh

4. _____

5. _____

How do you get to the park?

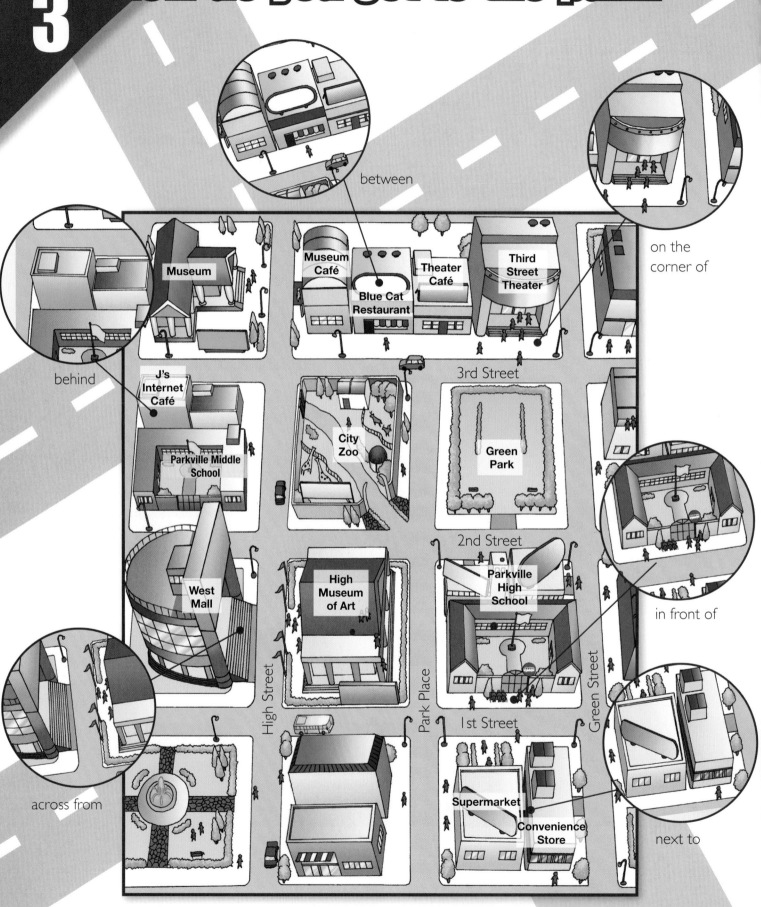

between

on the corner of

behind

Museum

Museum Café

Blue Cat Restaurant

Theater Café

Third Street Theater

3rd Street

J's Internet Café

City Zoo

Green Park

Parkville Middle School

2nd Street

in front of

West Mall

High Museum of Art

Parkville High School

across from

High Street

Park Place

1st Street

Green Street

Supermarket

Convenience Store

next to

Preview

Track 15

A Where are the people going? Listen to the conversations. Number the places in the order you hear them.

a. _____ bus stop   c. _____ restaurant   e. _____ Internet café

b. _____ theater   d. _____ mall   f. _____ convenience store

Track 15

B Listen again. Match one sentence to each place. Find the places on the map to check your answers.

a. It's next to the supermarket.
b. It's in front of the high school.
c. It's behind the middle school.
d. It's between Theater Café and Museum Café.
e. It's on the corner of Third Street and Green Street.
f. It's across from the Museum of Art.

- Internet café
- convenience store
- mall
- restaurant
- bus stop
- theater

C Point to the map. Ask a partner about each place.

A: What can you do at the supermarket?   B: You can buy food.

Conversation

Track 16

A Listen to the conversation. Then listen again and repeat.

B Practice the conversation with a partner. Replace the words in blue.

① Excuse me. Can you help me?

Sure. Where do you want to go?

No problem
Of course

② I want to go to the **museum of art**.

Thanks!

Hmm. It's on **High Street**. It's across from the mall.

Blue Cat Restaurant / Third Street
movie theater / Green Street

③ Can I help you?

Uh, yes, please. I'm looking for **the art museum.**

the restaurant
the theater

④ High Museum of Art

That's easy. It's right **behind** you!

It is? Oh, thanks!

in front of
next to

Language Focus

Track 17

A Look at the map below and study the chart.

How do you **get to** the park?	**Go straight down** Main Street.
	Go past the Internet café.
	Turn right **on** First Avenue.
	It's on the left.

B Look at the map again. Then number the directions in order.

1. I'm at the art museum. How do I get to the zoo?
   a. _____ It's on the right.
   b. _____ Turn left and go straight down Center Street.
   c. _____ Turn left on Main Street.
   d. _____ Turn right on 2nd Avenue.

2. Maya is at Kim's Restaurant. How does she get to the school?
   a. _____ Go past the art museum.
   b. _____ It's on the corner of 1st Avenue and Main Street.
   c. _____ Turn left on 1st Avenue.
   d. _____ Turn left and go straight down Center Street.

3. Stig and Ming are at the theater. How do they get to the mall?
   a. _____ Go past the art museum.
   b. _____ Turn left on Center Street.
   c. _____ Turn right and go straight down 2nd Avenue.
   d. _____ It's on 1st Avenue, across from the art museum.

Track 18

C Look again at the map above and complete the conversation. Then listen and check your answers.

Megan: I want to check my e-mail. Where can I get on the Internet?

Ted: Go to the 1st Avenue (1) _____. You can check your e-mail there.

Megan: How (2) _____ I _____ there from Mia's Pizza?

Ted: Turn right and go (3) _____ 3rd Avenue. Then (4) _____ on Main Street.

Megan: Uh, OK. Right on Main Street.

Ted: Right. Then (5) _____ the zoo. The Internet café is (6) _____. It's (7) _____ a Brazilian restaurant.

Megan: Great, thanks.

Pronunciation

Track 19

A Listen to the words. Then listen again and repeat.

O sounds

1. movie   2. go   3. front

Track 20

B Write the words in the chart. Then listen and check your answers.

| do   Tony's   no   open   come   two   London   oh |

Sounds like letter o in *movie*	Sounds like letter o in *go*	Sounds like letter o in *front*
do		

C Take turns reading the words in B with a partner.

Communication

Where are the places on the map. Student A looks at the city map below. Student B looks at the map on page 118. Ask and answer questions to complete the labels on your map.

Student A: Ask your partner for directions to the places below. Then label them on your map.

| museum   Internet café   movie theater   supermarket |

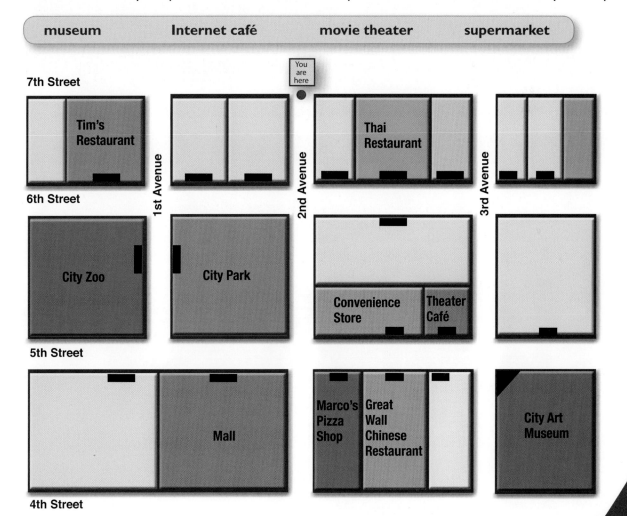

How do you get to the park?   **23**

Do you know?

Broadway, a street in New York City, is famous for its _____.

a. museums
b. schools
c. theaters

Reading

A Skim the article. What kind of city is Xi'an?

    a. an old city

    b. a modern city

    c. both an old and a modern city

B Read the article. Underline the different ways to travel.

C Answer the questions on page 26.

Xi'an, China

the Terracotta Army

city wall

ViSiT Xi'an!

Track 21

Xi'an is an amazing city in China. There are a lot of places to visit in the city, like museums, temples, and parks. Millions of visitors go to Xi'an every year. It is a very popular place to visit!

There is a huge 700-year-old wall around the city. You can walk or
5 ride a bike on the wall. Xi'an has other famous places, like the Museum of the Terracotta Army. It has a terracotta army with more than 8,000 soldiers. "Terracotta" is an Italian word. It means "cooked earth." The terracotta army is more than 2,200 years old! The museum is about 40 kilometers away from the city center. You can
10 take a train there.

The army is amazing. Each soldier looks different. There are short soldiers and tall soldiers. Some have beards (hair on their faces), and some don't. They are wearing different clothes.

Xi'an is an old city, but it is also very modern. There is an Internet
15 café in Xi'an with more than 3,000 computers!

25

Comprehension

A Answer the questions about *Visit Xi'an*!

1. This article is mainly about the _____ of Xi'an.

   a. people   b. places to visit   c. history

2. Which sentence about the city wall is NOT true?

   a. You can ride a bike on it.   b. It is very large and old.   c. It is next to the terracotta army.

3. How old are the terracotta soldiers?

   a. about 700 years old   b. about 2,200 years old   c. the article doesn't say

4. The Museum of the Terracotta Army is _____.

   a. in the city center   b. in the middle of the city   c. outside the city

5. What does "it" mean in line 14?

   a. the museum   b. Xi'an   c. China

Do you know ?

What or whom does the Terracotta Army protect?

a. an important person
b. a famous temple
c. an old city wall

B Sort these words into two categories.

| terracotta army | city wall | Internet café | terracotta soldier |
| computer | Internet | train | bicycle |

very old	modern

Writing

Read the travel brochure. Then make a walking tour of your neighborhood or town.

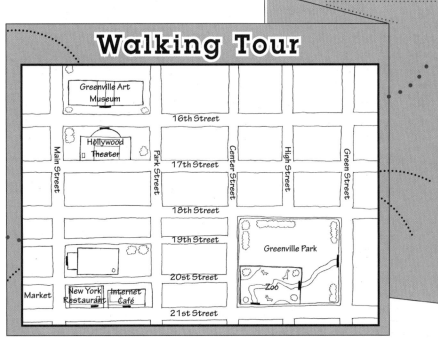

Walking Tour

Start at the art museum on the corner of 16th Street and Main Street. There are many famous paintings in the museum. Then go to the park. From the museum, go straight down 16th Street. Then take a right on Green Street. The park is on the right. Inside the park, there is a small zoo. Eat lunch at New York Restaurant on 21st Street. From the zoo, walk along 21st Street. Go past the Internet café on the corner of 21st Street and Park Street. The restaurant is next to the café. After lunch, see a movie at the old Hollywood Theater. Go straight down 21st Street and take a right on Main Street. Go straight on Main Street and take a right on 16th Street. The theater is on the right, across from the art museum.

The Real World

A Match the modes of transportation with the pictures.

1. ride a bus (30 km/h)
2. walk (5 km/h)
3. take a train / take the subway (60 km/h)
4. drive a car (50 km/h)
5. ride a bike (25 km/h)

(km/h = kilometers per hour)

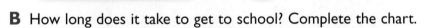

1

You can share a bike with everyone in Paris!

A service called Vélib' rents bikes to people from stations all over Paris. Vélib' has more than 20,500 bikes and 1,450 stations. To use the Vélib' bike service, you go to a station, pay, and take a bike. Then you return it to another station.

There are bike rental services like Vélib' in other cities in Europe and the United States. This service is cheap and saves energy!

Vélib' station

B How long does it take to get to school? Complete the chart.

	5 km
1. walk	(60 min ÷ 5 km/h) x 5 km = 60 minutes
2. bike	
3. bus	
4. car	
5. train/subway	

Idiom

"He drives me up the wall" means
_____.

a. He makes me angry
b. I like him
c. He is driving a car

New York City

"Hi! Do you want to see New York City? Come on! Let's take a tour!"

NEW JERSEY

Hudson River

CENTRAL PARK

W. 72ND ST.

CENTRAL PARK ST.

FIFTH AVENUE

PARK AVE.

THIRD AVE.

FIRST AVE.

E. 96TH ST.

E. 79TH ST.

E. 72ND ST.

TENTH AVENUE

W. 57TH ST.

CENTRAL PARK SOUTH

W. 42ND ST.

W. 34TH ST.

MANHATTAN

W. 23RD ST.

AVENUE OF THE AMERICAS

FIFTH AVENUE

S. PARK AVE.

THIRD AVENUE

FIRST AVE.

E. 57TH ST.

E. 42ND ST.

E. 34TH ST.

E. 14TH ST.

E. HOUSTON ST.

HUDSON STREET

BROADWAY

BOWERY

WEST STREET

PARK ROW

SOUTH STREET VIADUCT

QUEENSBORO BRIDGE

West Channel Chan.

East Channel

East River

WILLIAMSBURG BRIDGE

BROOKLYN

495

78

495

1 First, take a boat tour of New York Harbor from **Pier 83**. Look for the **Statue of Liberty** and famous buildings, like the Empire State Building.

2 From Pier 83, take a taxi to the **Museum of Natural History**. Learn about some amazing animals, take a trip to the moon, or travel 13 billion (13,000,000,000) years into the past!

3 **Central Park** is across from the museum. Walk through the park to the big lake and rent a boat. You can also run or ride a bike around the lake.

4 Walk across the park to the **Metropolitan Museum of Art** (the Met). See famous paintings from around the world, gold masks from Peru, and a real Egyptian temple. This statue of an Egyptian queen is more than 3,400 years old!

From the Met, **5** walk north one block, then walk east three blocks. Take the number 4 subway train south to **Grand Central Terminal**. About 700,000 people go to this famous train station every day!

Where is **New York**?

New York City (NYC) is in New York State, in the United States. The city has five parts, called boroughs. They are Manhattan, the Bronx, Brooklyn, Queens, and Staten Island.

New York City, United States

6 Don't miss **Times Square**! Walk west along 42nd Street to Times Square and watch a movie or eat great food. Then walk down Broadway and see a play at a theater.

Complete the notes with the words below.

watch a play
ride a bike
learn about animals
see famous paintings
take a train

Notes about **New York City**

1. Do you want to _____?
   Visit the Museum of Natural History.

2. You can _____ around the lake in Central Park.

3. The Metropolitan Museum of Art is a great place to _____.

4. You can _____ from Grand Central Terminal.

5. Visit Broadway and _____ at a theater.

 To learn more, watch the video **New York City**.

Unit 4
▶ Compare extreme places ▪
   around the world
▶ Talk about places you know ▪

Unit 5
▶ Compare cats and dogs, ▪
   and other animals
▶ Learn about animal language ▪

The Natural World

Unit 6
▶ Talk about past vacations ■
▶ Learn about an amazing adventure ■

UNIT 4
What's the coldest place on Earth?

North America

Europe

Asia

Africa

South America

Australia

Antarctica

Preview

Track 22

A Work with a partner and answer these questions. Then listen and check your ideas.

1. What's the hottest desert on Earth?	the Sahara	Antarctica
2. What's the largest river in the world?	the Amazon	the Nile
3. What's the highest mountain in the world?	the Amazon	Mt. Everest
4. What's the lowest place on Earth?	the Dead Sea	Antarctica
5. What's the coldest continent on Earth?	Antarctica	North America
6. What's the tallest waterfall in the world?	the Dead Sea	Angel Falls

Track 22

B Listen again. Write the number of each place (1–6) on the correct continent on the map.

C Label the pictures with your answers in A.

D Ask a partner questions about places you know.

    A: What's the largest park in New York City?   B: Central Park.

32   Unit 4

Conversation

A Listen to the conversation. Then listen again and repeat.

B Practice the conversation with a partner. Replace the words in **blue**.

> **Real English**
>
> Just a minute . . .

1 Can you help me study? I've got a geography test **tomorrow**.

Sure.

this afternoon
next week

2 OK. First question. What's the **coldest** continent in the world?

That's easy. Antarctica.

Right.

driest
windiest

3 Second question. What's the **highest mountain** on Earth?

Uh . . . **Mt. Everest**.

Good!

hottest desert / the Sahara
longest river / the Nile

4 OK. Here's your **last** question. What's the wettest place on Earth?

Just a minute, uh, the ocean?

Oh, Nadine!

third
next

Language Focus

Track 24

A Study the chart.

		big → the biggest
The Eiffel Tower is **the most famous** place in Paris.		rainy → the rainiest
What's **the driest** place on Earth?	**The driest** place on Earth is the Atacama Desert, in Chile.	famous → the most famous
What's **the longest** river in the world?	The Nile is **the longest** river in the world.	good → the best
		bad → the worst

B Complete the sentences with the correct form of the words given.

1. The _____ country in the world is Vatican City. (**small**)

2. Russia is the _____ country in the world. (**large**)

3. The _____ bird in the world is the bee hummingbird. (**tiny**)

4. Some people think that Atenas, Costa Rica, has the _____ weather in the world. (**good**)

5. Many people say that Paris is the _____ city in the world. (**beautiful**)

Track 25

C Make sentences using words from each column. Use each word only once. Then listen and check your answers.

the blue whale	dangerous	cave on Earth
the inland taipan	deep	trees in the world
redwoods	tall	animal in the world
Krubera Cave, Georgia	hot	place on Earth
Dakol, Ethiopia	heavy	snake in the world

Ethiopia

1. _____

2. _____

3. _____

4. _____

5. _____

the blue whale

Krubera Cave, Georgia

the inland taipan

redwoods

Pronunciation

Track 26

A Listen to the sentences. Then listen again and repeat.

Sentence Stress

1. The **Sahara** is the **hottest desert** in the **world**.

2. **What's** the **stormiest place** in **Asia**?

3. **Redwoods** are the **tallest trees** on **Earth**.

4. **What's** the **windiest place** in **North America**?

Do you know ?

The stormiest continent in the world is _____.
a. South America
b. Asia
c. Antarctica

Track 27

B Read the sentences and underline the important words. Then listen and circle the stressed words.

1. <u>Antarctica</u> is the <u>coldest</u> <u>place</u> on <u>Earth</u>.

2. What's the most famous city in Europe?

3. The Nile is the longest river in the world.

4. Mt. Everest is the tallest mountain on Earth.

5. Where's the tallest waterfall in South America?

6. The Amazon is the largest river in the world.

Communication

Form two groups and make a quiz. Each group writes ten questions. Then take turns asking and answering questions. Each correct question is one point. The team with the most points wins.

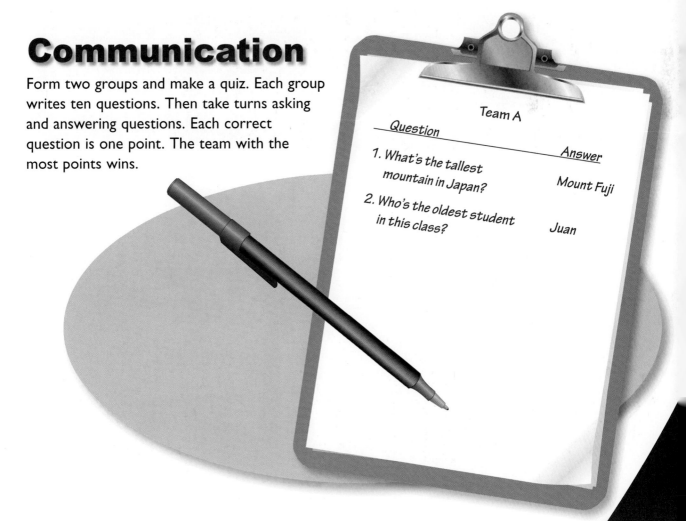

Team A

Question	Answer
1. What's the tallest mountain in Japan?	Mount Fuji
2. Who's the oldest student in this class?	Juan

Reading

A Skim the text. Then answer the question.

Why is the Amazon River important to the environment?

_____

_____

B Read the article. Underline the adjectives.

C Answer the questions on page 38.

The Amazon River, Brazil

anaconda

sloth

piranha

EXTREME AMAZON

Track 28

1 The Amazon is truly an extreme place.
Both the largest river and the largest
rain forest on Earth are in the Amazon.
The Amazon River starts in the Andes
5 Mountains in Peru and flows about 6,000
kilometers to the Atlantic Ocean. It is the
second longest river in the world. It is also
the largest river in the world. During the wet
season, parts of the river grow to 190 km wide!
10 Twenty percent of the fresh water in all the
world's oceans comes from the Amazon River.
Now that's extreme!

The Amazon River flows through the world's
largest rain forest. This rain forest has the
15 highest number of plants and animals on
Earth.
There are about 2.5 million kinds of insects
and 3,000 kinds of fish. One fifth of all
the birds in the world live in the Amazon. Some
20 animals in the rain forest are dangerous, but
others are not. There are scary animals, like
the meat-eating piranha and the anaconda, one
of the largest snakes in the world. But there
are also gentle animals, like the sloth. The
25 Amazon is very important for the environment.
Many people are trying to save the plants and
animals in the Amazon.

Amazon River

Amazon Rain Forest

SOUTH
AMERICA

Comprehension

A Answer the questions about *Extreme Amazon*.

1. What is the main idea of the text?
    a. A lot of interesting animals live in the rain forest.
    b. The Amazon River is very large and long.
    c. The Amazon is an extreme and important place.

2. The Amazon River is the _____ river in the world.
    a. longest   b. largest   c. most dangerous

3. The Amazon rain forest has more than two million kinds of _____.
    a. fish   b. birds   c. insects

4. The piranha is a kind of _____.
    a. snake   b. insect   c. fish

5. The _____ is a gentle animal.
    a. sloth   b. anaconda   c. piranha

Do you **know** ?

Green anacondas can grow to _____ meters.
a. 6
b. 9
c. 12

B Make a word web about the text.

the river — the Amazon — the rain forest

Writing

Read the poster. Then make a poster about your own city or country.

North

Chile

South

Extreme Chile!

Chile is the longest country in the world. It is 4,630 kilometers long from north to south.

The driest desert in the world, the Atacama Desert, is in Chile. In some places in the Atacama, there is no rain. In these places in the desert, plants and animals cannot live. The Atacama is also the highest desert in the world.

In the Atacama Desert, it is hot, dry, and sunny in summer. The temperature is about 27°C. In the winter, the temperature is about 22°C. It's warm and dry.

The Real World

What's the biggest city in the world?

A Which continent has the most people? Complete the chart with the numbers below.

10 m	21	24 m
4 b	1,000	4

Continent	Size (km²)	Number of people	People per km²
Asia	44 m		87
Africa	30 m	922 m	29
North America		529 m	22
South America	18 m	382 m	
Antarctica	14 m		0.00007
Europe		731 m	70
Australia	9 m	32 m	

1,000 = one thousand
1,000,000 = one million (m)
1,000,000,000 = one billion (b)

B Check your answers with a partner.

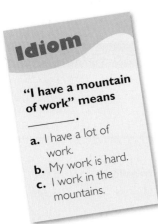

Idiom

"I have a mountain of work" means _____.

a. I have a lot of work.
b. My work is hard.
c. I work in the mountains.

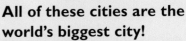

All of these cities are the world's biggest city!

▲ Including the city and the area around it, Tokyo, Japan, is the biggest city. There are over 35 million people living there.

▲ Mumbai, India, is the biggest city in the world. It has 14 million people living inside the city.

◀ Altamira, Brazil, is the biggest city in size. It covers 160,000 km².

Are cats cuter than dogs?

Preview

Track 29

A Listen to the conversation between Ramona and David. What do they think about cats and dogs? Circle **C** (for cats) or **D** (for dogs).

1. friendlier	C D	**5.** more playful	C D
2. gentler	C D	**6.** more intelligent	C D
3. more independent	C D	**7.** more dangerous	C D
4. cuter	C D	**8.** cleaner	C D

B What do you think about cats and dogs? Complete the chart using the words in A.

Cats are . . . than dogs.	Dogs are . . . than cats.
cleaner	

C Choose two animals and tell a partner about them. Take turns.

A: I think giraffes are gentler than elephants.
B: I disagree. I think elephants are gentler than giraffes.

pandas	monkeys	cats
giraffes	tigers	dogs
zebras	jaguars	elephants
rabbits	lions	rhinos

Conversation

Track 30

A Listen to the conversation. Then listen again and repeat.

B Practice the conversation with a partner. Replace the words in **blue**.

Real English

A spider?

1 I really want a **dog**.

Yeah, I love **dogs**.

cat / cats
pet rabbit / rabbits

2 Do you have a pet, Stig?

Yeah!

Yes, I do! He's really **friendly**. Do you want to see him?

playful
intelligent

3 He's really cool. He's **friendly**, but not as **friendly** as a spider.

gentle / gentle
intelligent / intelligent

A spider?

4 Here he is!

Oh! He's **a grasshopper**!

an insect
a bug

Are cats cuter than dogs? **41**

Language Focus

Track 31

A Study the chart.

Rabbits are **faster than** turtles.		big → bigger
Which is **more intelligent**, a tiger **or** an elephant?	An elephant is **more intelligent than** a tiger.	friendly → friendlier intelligent → more intelligent
Which is **faster**, a dog **or** a zebra?	**Neither**. A dog is **as fast as** a zebra.	good → better bad → worse
Spiders are dangerous, but lions are **more dangerous.**		
Spiders aren't **as dangerous as** lions.		

slower   faster

turtle   rabbit

B What do you think? Read the words in parentheses and make sentences. Use **–er** or **more . . . .**

1. <u>Grasshoppers are bigger than ants.</u>   (grasshoppers / big / ants)
2. _____   (dogs / friendly / cats)
3. _____   (cats / fast / rabbits)
4. _____   (dogs / intelligent / turtles)
5. _____   (penguins / good swimmers / pandas)
6. _____   (tigers / bad pets / dogs)

Track 32

C What do you think? Read the words in parentheses and make sentences. Use **as . . . as** or **not as . . . as**. Then listen. Does the speaker agree with you?

1. <u>Elephants aren't as large as whales.</u>   (elephants / large / whales)
2. <u>Penguins are as cute as dolphins.</u>   (penguins / cute / dolphins)
3. _____   (dolphins / dangerous / sharks)
4. _____   (cats / smart / dogs)
5. _____   (sharks / intelligent / dolphins)
6. _____   (sharks / scary / spiders)

dolphin

shark

whale

penguin

Pronunciation

Track 33

A Listen to the sentences. Then listen again and repeat.

Reduction: *than*

1. Dogs are friendlier than cats.
2. Dolphins are gentler than sharks.

Track 34

B Listen to the sentences. Write the missing words.

1. Lions are more intelligent ___*than hippos*___.
2. Cats are more independent _____.
3. Are giraffes taller _____?
4. Turtles are gentler _____.
5. Is a dog cuter _____?
6. I think lions are faster _____.

C Take turns reading the sentences in B with a partner.

Do you know?

Where do penguins NOT live?
a. South Africa
b. Canada
c. Antarctica

Communication

Play a chain game!

Student A chooses two animals and compares them.

Student B chooses one of Student A's animals and compares it to a new animal.

Take turns. If a student can't make a sentence, the other student gets one point.

A: I think cats are cuter than dogs.

B: Yes, but cats aren't as cute as rabbits.

A: That's true, and rabbits are friendlier than tigers.

B: But tigers are . . .

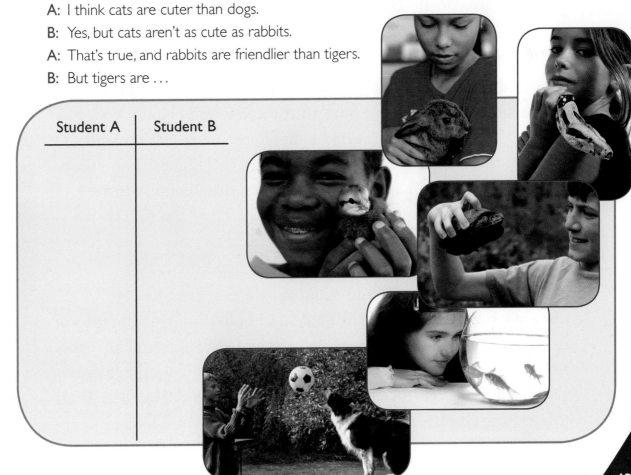

Student A	Student B

Are cats cuter than dogs?   **43**

Reading

A Look at the pictures and skim the text. What is the main idea of the article?

  a. Some dogs are smarter than other dogs.

  b. Dogs can help people.

  c. Golden retrievers are good pets.

  d. German shepherds help people in the snow.

B Read the article. Underline the words that compare different kinds of dogs.

C Answer the questions on page 46.

Working Dogs

Track 35

1   Dogs are great pets. They're loyal, playful, and intelligent. But some dogs are smarter than others. These smart dogs help people. They are working dogs.

    Rescue dogs can help people who are lost. They can find people
5   in the mountains, in the desert, in the snow, and even in water. Rescue dogs are usually German shepherds or Saint Bernards, because these dogs are stronger and more intelligent than other dogs. German shepherds and other rescue dogs usually have better ears and noses than other dogs, too. They can find things
10 and people. Saint Bernards usually work in the snow. They have a lot of fur to keep them warm in cold weather.

    Some people cannot see, and some people cannot hear. Guide dogs can help these people at home and help them go outside. For example, guide dogs guide people as they turn right and left, and
15 help them stop at street corners. Guide dogs are usually golden or Labrador retrievers, because they are gentler and friendlier than other dogs. Guide dogs can help people have normal lives.

Saint Bernard

Labrador retriever

German shepherd

Comprehension

A Answer the questions about *Working Dogs*.

1. Rescue dogs are _____ than other dogs.

   a. faster   **b.** larger   **c.** smarter

2. Why are rescue dogs good at finding people?

   a. They are friendlier than other dogs.   **b.** They have good ears and noses.   **c.** They are loyal and playful.

3. What can we infer from the second paragraph?

   a. All dogs can be guide dogs.

   b. Some rescue dogs can swim.

   c. Rescue dogs are often dangerous.

4. Good guide dogs are _____.

   a. gentle   **b.** independent   **c.** cute

5. Guide dogs are usually _____.

   a. German shepherds   **b.** Saint Bernards   **c.** Labrador or golden retrievers

Do you know?

What's the smartest kind of dog?
a. German shepherd
b. golden retriever
c. border collie

B Complete the sentences comparing the working dogs to other dogs.

1. German shepherds and Saint Bernards are _____.

2. German shepherds and Saint Bernards have _____.

3. Golden and Labrador retrievers are _____.

Writing

Read the blog post. Then write a blog post about your favorite pet or animal.

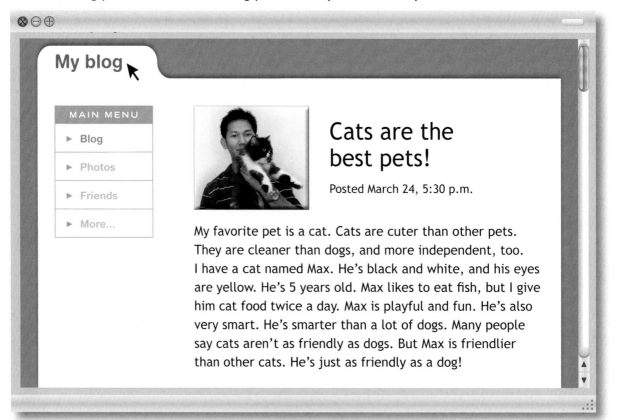

My blog

MAIN MENU
▶ Blog
▶ Photos
▶ Friends
▶ More...

Cats are the best pets!

Posted March 24, 5:30 p.m.

My favorite pet is a cat. Cats are cuter than other pets. They are cleaner than dogs, and more independent, too. I have a cat named Max. He's black and white, and his eyes are yellow. He's 5 years old. Max likes to eat fish, but I give him cat food twice a day. Max is playful and fun. He's also very smart. He's smarter than a lot of dogs. Many people say cats aren't as friendly as dogs. But Max is friendlier than other cats. He's just as friendly as a dog!

The Real World

Cats and dogs can't talk. They meow and bark, but we can't really understand what they are saying. But cats and dogs have expressions, just like people! We can guess what cats and dogs are feeling when we look at their face, ears, body, and tail. When cats are alert, their eyes are big. Their ears and tail are up. When dogs are afraid, they look down. Their head and tail are low. Their ears are down. The dog is saying, "I'm afraid."

What are these animals saying? Circle the correct words under the pictures.

body

head

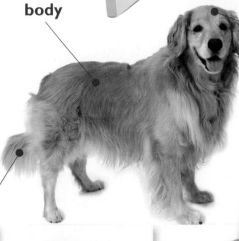

tail

Idiom

"It's raining cats and dogs" means
_____.

a. it's raining a lot
b. it's raining a little
c. there are a lot of cats and dogs outside

1. sad   alert

2. angry   playful

3. happy   afraid

4. curious   sad

5. alert   angry

6. playful   afraid

7. alert   sad

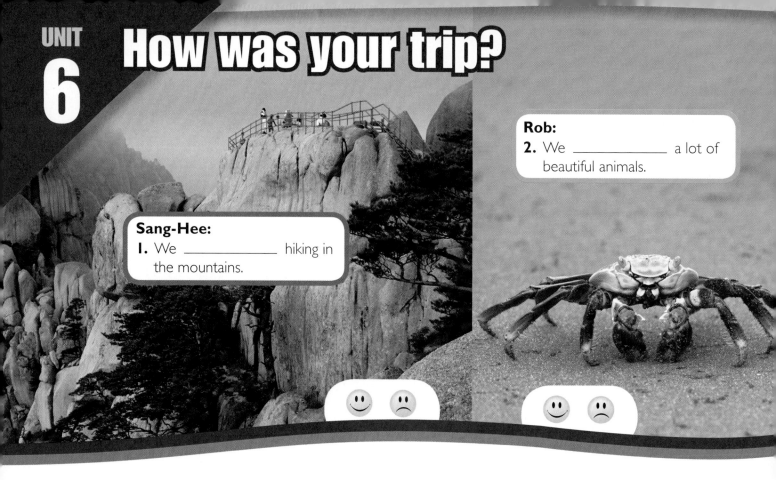

How was your trip?

Rob:
2. We _____ a lot of beautiful animals.

Sang-Hee:
1. We _____ hiking in the mountains.

Preview

Track 36

A Some teenagers are talking about their trips. Complete the sentences about what the students did.

> took   went   ate   saw   swam

Track 36

B Listen again. Did they have a good time or a bad time? Listen and circle ☺ or ☹.

C Who had the best trip? Who had the worst trip? Tell a partner.

   A: I think Rob had the best trip.

   B: I disagree. I think Michiko had the best trip.

D What was your best trip? Complete the chart and tell your partner about your trip.

Where did you go?	When did you go?	More information
I went to Thailand.	summer, 2008	It was hot and sunny.

Maria
3. We _____ in the ocean.

Frances:
4. We _____ a lot of interesting food.

Michiko:
5. We _____ a boat trip.

Conversation

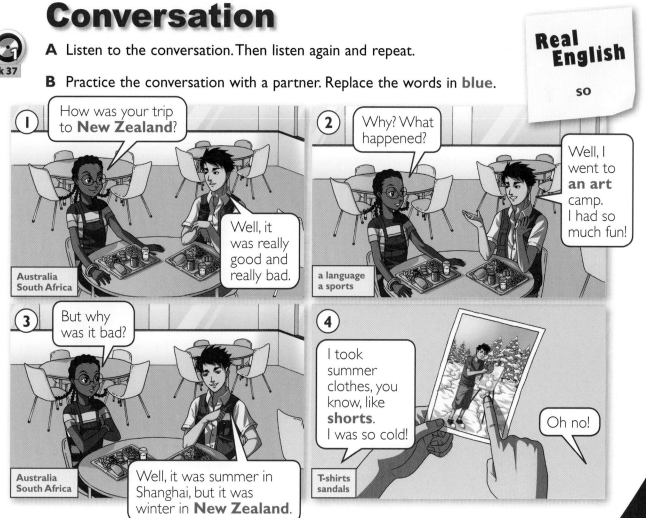

Track 37

A Listen to the conversation. Then listen again and repeat.

B Practice the conversation with a partner. Replace the words in blue.

1. How was your trip to **New Zealand**?

   Well, it was really good and really bad.

   Australia
   South Africa

2. Why? What happened?

   Well, I went to **an art** camp. I had so much fun!

   a language
   a sports

3. But why was it bad?

   Well, it was summer in Shanghai, but it was winter in **New Zealand**.

   Australia
   South Africa

4. I took summer clothes, you know, like **shorts**. I was so cold!

   Oh no!

   T-shirts
   sandals

Language Focus

Track 38

A Study the chart.

Where **did** you **go** on vacation?	I **went** to Bali. I **got** a cool mask.	be → was / were
How **was** her trip?	It **was** fantastic! She **had** a great time.	visit → visited
		like → liked
What **did** you **see** on your trip?	We **saw** a lot of amazing animals.	stay → stayed
		study → studied
Did he **visit** a temple?	No, he **didn't**, but he **visited** a lot of museums.	stop → stopped

B What did the students do on their vacation? Complete the sentences.

1. Jun _____ a lot of interesting paintings at the art museum. (**see**)
2. Clara _____ a train to Mexico City. (**take**)
3. Ana _____ to the beach and _____ in the ocean. (**go** / **swim**)
4. Carlos and John _____ some temples in Osaka, Japan. (**visit**)
5. Jenny _____ home and _____ English. (**stay** / **study**)
6. Ben _____ to Thailand and _____ a lot of delicious food. (**go** / **eat**)

Track 39

C Ethan is talking to Jamie about his vacation. Complete the dialog with the correct form of the verbs in the box. Then listen and check your answers.

take	swim	climb	get
go	do	be	go

Jamie: How (1) _____ your vacation, Ethan?

Ethan: It was great. I (2) _____ to the mountains with my family.

Jamie: Really? What (3) _____ you _____ there?

Ethan: Well, we (4) _____ hiking. It was so beautiful.

Jamie: How (5) _____ you _____ there?

Ethan: We (6) _____ a train, then we (7) _____ up the mountain.

Jamie: What else did you do?

Ethan: We (8) _____ in a river. It was fun, but the water was so cold!

Pronunciation

Track 40

A Listen to the sentences. Then listen again and repeat.

Regular past tense verb ending: -ed sounds

1. They **stayed** in a great place.	**d**
2. We **liked** the boat trip a lot.	**t**
3. She **visited** the museum.	**id**

Track 41

B Which sounds do the verbs have? Listen and circle the sound.

1. We watched a play at a temple.	**d**	**t**	**id**
2. It snowed a lot during the trip.	**d**	**t**	**id**
3. I wanted to take a fun vacation.	**d**	**t**	**id**
4. The train stopped at the station.	**d**	**t**	**id**
5. He climbed up Mt. Everest.	**d**	**t**	**id**
6. They learned English at school.	**d**	**t**	**id**

C Take turns reading the sentences in B with a partner.

Do you know?

The highest part of a mountain is called the

_____.

a. rock
b. summit
c. cliff

Communication

A Work in a small group. Take turns asking each student questions about a trip he or she made. Remember the answers.

B Say as much as possible about the other students in your group. Who can remember the most things?

Where did you go on vacation?

I went to Finland.

Reading

A Scan the text. How is Erden Eruç traveling around the world? Circle the words.

taking a train	riding a bike	taking a plane	driving a car
rowing a boat	walking	climbing	taking a bus

B Read the text and circle the distances. Then write them out in words.

1. _one hundred and eight kilometers_

2. _____

3. _____

4. _____

C Answer the questions on page 54.

Erden riding his bike

Erden on Mt. McKinley

Around and Over the World

Erden Eruç is no ordinary adventurer. He wants to climb, hike, ride, and row around the world using only human power.

Erden, a Turkish-American man, started his journey in the United States on February 1, 2003. He rode his bike from Seattle to Alaska. Then he hiked 108 km to Mt. McKinley— the highest mountain in North America at 6,194 m—and climbed to the top with his friends. Then Erden rode back to Seattle. He rode 8,925 km in 204 days!

Next, in 2005 and 2006, Erden rowed across the Atlantic Ocean alone in his small 7.1-meter boat. He rowed 7,334 km from Lisbon, Portugal, to the Caribbean Sea. He reached Guadeloupe on May 5, 2006.

After that, in 2007 and 2008, Erden rowed 15,166 km across the Pacific Ocean from Bodega Bay in California to Papua New Guinea. He rowed more than 10 hours every day for 312 days—that's a world record!

During his boat trips, Erden saw sharks and other amazing fish. Birds visited his boat, too. At night, Erden went into a little room on the boat. There he wrote in his diary, called his friends, and surfed the Internet.

Why is Erden making this human-powered journey? One reason is to teach children. Erden is visiting schools around the world. He wants every child to have a goal in life. Erden says life is difficult sometimes, but it's an adventure, too.

Comprehension

A Answer the questions about *Around and Over the World*.

1. What is the highest mountain in the United States?

    a. Alaska   **b.** Everest   **c.** McKinley

2. How many kilometers did Erden travel across the Atlantic Ocean?

    a. 7,334   **b.** 8,925   **c.** 15,166

3. Which journey was a world record?

    a. his journey across the Pacific

    b. his journey across the Atlantic

    c. his journey from Seattle to Alaska

4. We can infer that Erden took a _____ on his boat.

    a. friend   **b.** bike   **c.** computer

5. What does Erden mean when he says that life is an adventure?

    a. He likes to travel.   **b.** He thinks life is exciting.   **c.** He thinks life is dangerous.

Do you **know**?

Which is the largest ocean in the world?

a. The Pacific Ocean
b. The Atlantic Ocean
c. The Indian Ocean

B This chart shows information about three of Erden's journeys.
Which items can you find in the reading? Circle them.

	Seattle → Mt. McKinley → Seattle	Lisbon → Guadeloupe	Bodega Bay → Papua New Guinea
Days	204	176	312
Start	February 1, 2003	November 9, 2005	July 10, 2007
Finish	August 24, 2003	May 5, 2006	May 17, 2008
Distance	8,925 km	7,334 km	15,166 km

Writing

Read the e-mail. Then write an e-mail about a trip you took.

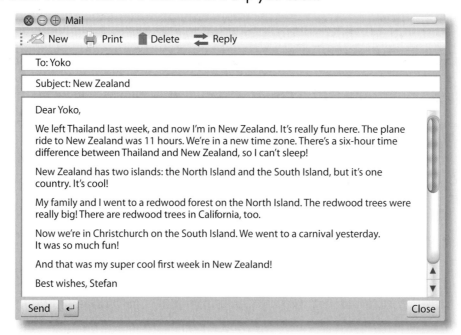

⊗ ⊖ ⊕ Mail

✉ New   🖨 Print   🗑 Delete   ⇄ Reply

To: Yoko

Subject: New Zealand

Dear Yoko,

We left Thailand last week, and now I'm in New Zealand. It's really fun here. The plane ride to New Zealand was 11 hours. We're in a new time zone. There's a six-hour time difference between Thailand and New Zealand, so I can't sleep!

New Zealand has two islands: the North Island and the South Island, but it's one country. It's cool!

My family and I went to a redwood forest on the North Island. The redwood trees were really big! There are redwood trees in California, too.

Now we're in Christchurch on the South Island. We went to a carnival yesterday. It was so much fun!

And that was my super cool first week in New Zealand!

Best wishes, Stefan

Send   ↵   Close

The Real World

What are the Seven Summits?

Look at the map of the United States. The map has a scale. Use the scale to find out about how far away these places are from each other.

The Seven Summits are the highest mountains on each of the seven continents. These mountains are very difficult to climb. People practice for many years before they climb them. The youngest person to climb the Seven Summits is Johnny Strange. He was 17 when he achieved his goal. The oldest person is Ramón Blanco. He completed the summits one week before his 74th birthday!

Erden Eruç is climbing six of the Seven Summits. He climbed Mt. McKinley in 2003. He wants to climb Kosciuszko, Everest, Elbrus, Kilimanjaro, and Aconcagua as part of his "around and over the world" trip.

	Seattle	Bodega Bay	Chicago	New Orleans
Seattle		1,000		
Bodega Bay				
Chicago				
New Orleans				

Continent	Summit	Height (meters)
Africa	Kilimanjaro	5,895
Antarctica	Vinson	4,897
Australia	Kosciuszko	2,228
Asia	Everest	8,848
Europe	Elbrus	5,642
North America	McKinley	6,194
South America	Aconcagua	6,962

Idiom

"She talks a mile a minute" means
_____.

a. she talks very fast.
b. she talks very slow.
c. she talks in a loud voice.

Antarctica

Antarctica is the wildest place on Earth! Tourists usually visit here for only a few days, and scientists stay for a few months in the summer. But emperor penguins live here all year round!

▲ Scientists from all over the world work in Antarctica. These scientists are studying the Antarctic sea ice.

◄ Some people like to climb the mountains in Antarctica. This climber is on a mountain called Pyramid Peak.

Cold—Colder—Coldest!

Antarctica is a land of extremes. It is:

- the **coldest** continent. The lowest temperature ever recorded here was −89.2°C at Vostok Station in 1983.
- the **darkest** continent. There is no sunlight for six months of the year.
- the **driest** continent. Less than 5 cm of rain or snow fall every year.
- the **highest** continent. The average height above sea level is 2,500 m.
- the **windiest** continent. Strong winds can blow 300 km per hour.

56

Emperor penguins

. . . are amazing animals—and they're great parents, too!

The mother emperor penguin lays one egg each year in the winter. She then goes to the sea to look for food. Sometimes the sea is more than 80 km away! The father keeps the egg warm on his feet.

For two months, the father doesn't eat. In the spring, the mother returns with food. The baby penguin comes out of its egg. Then the father goes to the sea to look for more food. He's really hungry!

Emperor penguin facts

Height:	115 cm
Weight:	Up to 40 kg
Life:	15–20 years
Food:	small fish

Where is **Antarctica**?

Antarctica is the world's most southern continent.

Antarctica

Can penguins fly?

No, they can't, but they are great swimmers.

▼ **Circle the correct words to complete the notes.**

Notes about **Antarctica**

1. Antarctica is the (*southernmost* / *northernmost*) continent in the world.

2. The coldest temperature in Antarctica was about (*-89°C* / *-98°C*) in 1983.

3. There is no sunlight for (*two* / *six*) months of the year.

4. Emperor penguins (*can* / *can't*) swim.

5. Emperor penguin (*mothers* / *fathers*) don't eat for two months in the winter.

 To learn more, watch the video *Antarctica*.

Review Game 1

Play with 2–4 people. Take turns. Each person has a game counter. Toss a coin and move your counter. The first person to finish is the winner!

START

1 Say three things you like to do on weekends.

2 Who is the tallest person in your class?

3 It is the coldest continent on Earth.

4 Describe how this person is feeling.

5 How often do you browse the Internet?

6 Describe someone in your class. The other players guess who it is.

7 What does "keep a straight face" mean?

8 Give directions from your house to school.

9 It is a city in the U.S. with five boroughs.

10 Say where one store and one restaurant are where you live.

11 It is an ancient walled city in China.

12 What does "he drives me up the wall" mean?

13 Say three things you did last summer.

Heads = move two squares   **Tails** = move one square

Red: Answer the question.   **Blue:** Follow the instruction.
Green: Ask the question. For example, when you read, "It is the world's highest mountain," ask, *What is Mt. Everest?*

Can't answer? Miss a turn!

FINISH

25 Name four animals that are faster than a turtle.

24 It's a bird. It can't fly, but it's a great swimmer!

23 What does "she talks a mile a minute" mean?

22 Name two things that working dogs can do.

21 It is the heaviest animal in the world.

20 Name four modes of transportation.

19 What are the Seven Summits?

14 It is a martial art, a dance, and a game.

15 Compare two animals. Say three things.

16 What animal does Ming really want?

17 It is the largest river in the world.

18 Say three things about Antarctica.

59

Communication: Student B Activities

Unit 3

Student B: Ask your partner for directions to the places below. Then label them on your map.

Chinese restaurant   art museum   zoo   convenience store

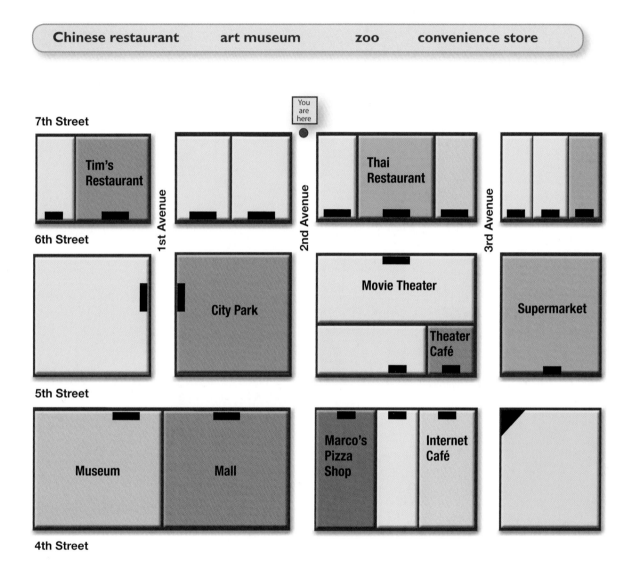

Irregular Past Tense Verbs

Base form	Past form
become	became
bring	brought
buy	bought
catch	caught
choose	chose
come	came
cost	cost
cut	cut
draw	drew
drink	drank
drive	drove
eat	ate
fall	fell
feel	felt
fight	fought
find	found
fly	flew
get	got
give	gave
go	went
grow	grew
hear	heard
hurt	hurt
keep	kept
know	knew
let	let

Base form	Past form
lose	lost
make	made
mean	meant
meet	met
pay	paid
put	put
read	read
ride	rode
run	ran
say	said
see	saw
sell	sold
show	showed
sing	sang
sleep	slept
speak	spoke
swim	swam
take	took
teach	taught
tell	told
think	thought
throw	threw
understand	understood
wear	wore
win	won
write	wrote

Language Notes

► UNIT 1 What do you like to do?

like + infinitive

What do	you they	like to do?	I They	like to don't like to	draw.
What does	he she		He She	likes to doesn't like to	play sports.

Wh- Questions (*How often*)

How often do	you they	play basketball?	I They	**play** once a week.
How often does	he she		He She	**plays** twice a week.

Time Expressions

once twice three times four times five times six times	a week a month a year	on	Mondays Tuesdays Wednesdays Thursdays Fridays Saturdays Sundays weekdays weekends
every day			

► UNIT 2 What does she look like?

look like

What **do**	you they	look like?	I'm They're	tall.
			I **have** They **have**	long brown hair.
What **does**	he she		He's She's	medium height.
			He **wears** She **wears**	glasses.

Adjectival Order

Size	Style	Color	Body Part
long short	curly spiky straight	black blond brown red	hair
		blue brown green gray	eyes

▶ UNIT 3   How do you get to the park?

Prepositions of Location

Where is the museum?	It's	**across from** the park. **behind** the museum. **in front of** the restaurant. **next to** the zoo.
		on the corner of First Street and Second Street.
		between the park **and** the zoo.

Imperatives (Directions)

| How do you get to the park? | **Go straight down** Main Street.
Go past the Internet café.
Turn left/right on First Avenue.
It's **on the left/right**. |

▶ UNIT 4 What's the coldest place on Earth?

Superlative Adjectives

Short adjectives (1 syllable)	high low	**the** high**est** **the** low**est**
1-syllable adjectives (ending with a short vowel sound and a single consonant)	big hot	**the** big**gest** **the** hot**test**
Adjectives ending in -y	rainy windy	**the** rain**iest** **the** wind**iest**
Longer adjectives (2 or more syllables)	famous dangerous	**the most** famous **the most** dangerous
Irregular adjectives	good bad	**the best** **the worst**

▶ UNIT 5 Are cats cuter than dogs?

Wh- Questions (*Which*)—Comparative Adjectives

Short adjectives (1 syllable)	clean cute	clean**er than** cut**er than**
1-syllable adjectives (ending with a short vowel sound and a single consonant)	big hot	big**ger than** hot**ter than**
Adjectives ending in -y	friendly scary	friend**lier than** scar**ier than**
Longer adjectives (2 or more syllables)	intelligent	**more** intelligent **than** **less** intelligent **than**
Irregular adjectives	good bad	**better than** **worse than**

Comparatives (as . . . as)

Some tigers are **as big as** lions.

Sharks aren't **as intelligent as** dolphins.

▶ UNIT 6 How was your trip?

Simple Past Regular Verbs

Most verbs, add -ed	visit stay	visit**ed** stay**ed**
Verbs that have 1 syllable, a short vowel sound, and end with a single consonant	stop	stop**ped**
Verbs that end with a consonant + y	study	stud**ied**

Simple Past Irregular Verbs (Be)

I **was**
you **were**
he **was**
she **was**
it **was**
we **were**
they **were**

Simple Past Irregular Verbs

do	**did**
eat	**ate**
get	**got**
go	**went**
have	**had**
ride	**rode**
see	**saw**
swim	**swam**
take	**took**
write	**wrote**

Simple Past Information Questions

How	**was**	your trip?
	were	the museums?

What **did**	you he she they	**do** on vacation?
Where **did**		**go**?
Did		**visit** a temple?

Simple Past Statements

I He	**went** to Paris.
She They	**didn't go** to New York.

Language Notes **125**

Vocabulary Index

Credits

PHOTO CREDITS

Page iii: NASA; **vi–vii:** (clockwise from dog) Jean Frooms/iStockphoto, Michael Fay/National Geographic Image Collection, Gary Martin/iStockphoto, MaxFX/Shutterstock, Lagui/Shutterstock, Birgit Prentner/iStockphoto, Phil Schofield/National Geographic Image Collection, Joselito Briones/iStockphoto, Lucian Coman/Shutterstock, Jan Martin Will/Shutterstock, O. Louis Mazzatenta/National Geographic Image Collection, sgame/Shutterstock; **2–3:** Michael S. Yamashita/National Geographic Image Collection; **2:** (l) Hemis/Alamy, (r) Michael Nichols/National Geographic Image Collection; **3:** iStockphoto; **4–5:** (l to r) Jacek Chabraszewski/Shutterstock, Judy McPhail/iStockphoto, H. Rumph, Jr./AP Images, Judi Ashlock/iStockphoto, Linda Kloosterhof/iStockphoto; **7:** sgame/Shutterstock; **8–9:** Hemis/Alamy; **8:** SPP Images/Alamy; **10:** Lucian Coman/Shutterstock; **11:** (tl) George Peters/iStockphoto, (tr) Steven Pumphrey/National Geographic Image Collection, (b) Cheryl L. Opperman/National Geographic Image Collection; **12–13:** (l to r) iStockphoto, Zhang Bo/iStockphoto, Isabelle Limbach/iStockphoto, iStockphoto, Miroslav Ferkuniak/iStockphoto; **14:** (1) Jaroslaw Wojcik/iStockphoto, (2) Jaroslaw Wojcik/iStockphoto, (3) Justin Horrocks/iStockphoto, (4) Pathathai Chungyam/iStockphoto, (5 & 6) iStockphoto; **15:** Photos 12/Alamy; **16–17:** J. D. Heaton/AGE Fotostock; **16:** (l) Jeff Garner/Southern Illinois University, Carbondale, (r) Lagui/Shutterstock; **19:** (1) Shelly Perry/iStockphoto, (2) Rasmus Rasmussen/iStockphoto, (3) Juan Estey/iStockphoto, (4) Erics/Shutterstock, (5) Joselito Briones/iStockphoto; **24–25:** O. Louis Mazzatenta/National Geographic Image Collection; **25:** Nataliya Hora/iStockphoto; **27:** (t, l to r) Jane Norton/iStockphoto, Paul Kline/iStockphoto, Jacek Chabraszewski/iStockphoto (b, l to r) iStockphoto, Steve Geer/iStockphoto, Joerg Reimann/iStockphoto; **28:** (l) ExaMedia Photography/Shutterstock, (r) Michael S. Yamashita/National Geographic Image Collection; **29:** (tl) Kenneth Garrett/National Geographic Image Collection, (tr) Ira Block/National Geographic Image Collection, (b) Gary718/Shutterstock; **30–31:** Alaska Stock Images/National Geographic Image Collection; **30:** (l) Kevin Schafer/National Geographic Image Collection, (r) Mark Raycroft/Minden Pictures/National Geographic Image Collection; **31:** Photo courtesy Doug Gilmour; **32–33:** (1) Birgit Prentner/iStockphoto, (2) Michael Fay/National Geographic Image Collection, (3) Jörg Jahn/Shutterstock, (4) Magicinfoto/Shutterstock, (5) Frontpage/Shutterstock, (6) Armin Rose/Shutterstock; **34:** (t) Michael Dodd/iStockphoto, (m) WellyWelly/Shutterstock, (bl) Flip Nicklin/Minden Pictures/National Geographic Image Collection, (bm) Stephen Alvarez/National Geographic Image Collection, (br) Jason Edwards/National Geographic Image Collection; **36–37:** Johnny Lye/Shutterstock; **36:** (tl) Thomas Marent/Minden Pictures/National Geographic Image Collection, (tr) Michael Durham/Minden Pictures/National Geographic Image Collection, (b) Paul Zahl/National Geographic Image Collection; **38:** Thomas Marent/Minden Pictures/National Geographic Image Collection; **39:** (t) Sam DCruz/Shutterstock, (m) Simon Webber/iStockphoto, (b) Esteban Felix/AP Images; **40–41:** Mehmet Salih Guler/iStockphoto; **42:** (l to r) Tom C. Amon/Shutterstock, Mike Parry/Minden Pictures/National Geographic Image Collection, Flip Nicklin/National Geographic Image Collection, Jan Martin Will/Shutterstock; **43:** (clockwise from tl) iStockphoto, Rebecca Abell/Shutterstock, iStockphoto, Carmen Martínez Banús/iStockphoto, Annette Wiechmann/iStockphoto, Denice Breaux/iStockphoto; **44–45:** Jim Parkin/iStockphoto; **45:** (t) Atref/Shutterstock, (b) Jim Craigmyle/Corbis; **46:** Ronen/Shutterstock; **47:** (t) Lisa Svara/iStockphoto, (1) David Ward/Getty Images, (2) Igor Grochev/iStockphoto, (3) Wallace Garrison/Photolibrary, (4) Jean Frooms/iStockphoto, (5) Stockbyte/SuperStock, (6) David Ward/Getty Images, (7) Milena Sobieraj/iStockphoto; **48–49:** (l to r) Christophe Boisvieux/Corbis, Gary Martin/iStockphoto, Rihards Plivch/iStockphoto, Loic Bernard/iStockphoto, JTB Photo Communications/AGE Fotostock; **52–53:** Photo credit Terry Schmitt; **52:** (both) Photo courtesy Erden Eruç; **56:** (l) Gordon Wiltsie/National Geographic Image Collection, (r) Maria Stenzel/National Geographic Image Collection; **57:** (t) Maria Stenzel/National Geographic Image Collection, (b, both) Ralph Lee Hopkins/National Geographic Image Collection; **58–59:** Vladimir Wrangel/Shutterstock; **58:** (tl) Joselito Briones/iStockphoto, (tr) Craig Kassover/National Geographic Image Collection, (bl) ExaMedia Photography/Shutterstock, (br) Hemis/Alamy; **59:** (t) Atref/Shutterstock, (b) Maria Stenzel/National Geographic Image Collection.

ART CREDITS

WORKBOOK 2

Carmella Lieske

HEINLE
CENGAGE Learning

Australia • Brazil • Japan • Korea • Mexico • Singapore • Spain • United Kingdom • United States

What do you like to do?

Vocabulary Focus

Match the pictures to the words.

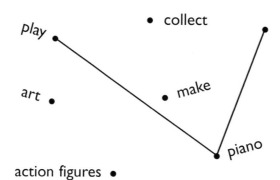

play   • collect

art •   • make

• piano

action figures •

• animals

practice •

• martial arts

draw •

Conversation

Put the conversation in the correct order from 1 to 8. Then practice with a partner at school.

a. ___1___ Hi, Susana! Do you like to play sports?

b. _____ Um . . . that's OK, Peter. What else do you like to do?

c. _____ Uh-huh, I can play the piano for you.

d. _____ Oh, cool, and I can teach you soccer.

e. _____ Well, on the weekends, I like to draw.

f. _____ Wow! Do you play a musical instrument?

g. _____ Well, I like to draw, too! Let's take an art class together!

h. _____ Hi, Peter. No, I don't like sports, but I like to play music.

Language Focus

A Circle the correct words to complete the conversation. Then practice with two partners at school.

Mr. Brown: Hello. My name's Mr. Brown. I (**like** / likes) to make art. (**Do** / Does) you?

Dave: I love to (**draw** / draws) pictures. (**Do** / Does) you like to draw, Mr. Brown?

Mr. Brown: Yes, I (**do** / does). I (**like** / likes) to paint, too.

Dave: (How many / **How often**) do you draw?

Mr. Brown: I (**draw** / draws) every morning, before school. What do you do after school, Kelly?

Kelly: Well . . . sometimes I (**play** / plays) soccer with my sister. She (play / **plays**) soccer three times a week.

Mr. Brown: I like to (**play** / plays) soccer, too! Our team (**practice** / practices) every Tuesday.

B Look at the timetable. Answer the questions.

	Monday	Tuesday	Wednesday	Thursday	Friday	Saturday & Sunday
Before School	**Ben:** soccer	**Ben:** soccer	**Sandra:** guitar	**Ben:** soccer	**Ben:** soccer	**Ben and Sandra:** piano
After School	**Sandra:** karate	**Ben:** art class	**Sandra:** karate	**Sandra:** art class	**Sandra:** karate	

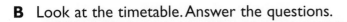

1. When does Ben play soccer? How often?

_____

2. How often does Sandra do karate? When?

_____

3. When does Sandra play the guitar?

_____

4. When do they play the piano?

_____

Reading

A Scan the article. What sports does Jintao talk about?

1. _____ 2. _____ 3. _____

Meet the Team!

This is Jintao. He's on the baseball team.

What do you like to do after school?

Jintao: After school, I usually play baseball. I love to play
baseball. This is a picture of our team. My best friend, Yong Ming,
is on the team, too. In the spring and summer, we play baseball
before school every day, too. In the fall, we only play baseball
after school on weekdays. But in the winter, I play basketball
after school, and he plays tennis. It's too cold to go outside.

What else do you like to do?

Jintao: Well . . . I like to watch movies on weekends. I really
like martial arts movies. They're cool. Once a month, I go to a
street market and buy a new action figure. I collect **them**. I have
about 50.

B Read the article in **A**. Answer the questions.

1. When does Jintao usually play baseball?

   a. after school   **b.** before school   **c.** before and after school

2. Who is Yong Ming?

   a. Jintao's teacher   **b.** Jintao's brother   **c.** Jintao's best friend

3. When does Jintao NOT play baseball?

   a. in the spring   **b.** in the fall   **c.** in the winter

4. What other sport does Jintao play?

   a. baseball   **b.** basketball   **c.** tennis

5. What does the "them" in blue refer to?

   a. baseballs   **b.** action figures   **c.** movies

C Answer the questions.

1. What do you like to do after school? _____

2. Do you like to practice martial arts? _____

3. How often do you watch movies? _____

Writing

A What do you do before and after school? Complete the timetable.

	Monday	Tuesday	Wednesday	Thursday	Friday	Saturday & Sunday
Before School						
After School						

B Using the information in **A**, write an e-mail to a friend about your timetable.

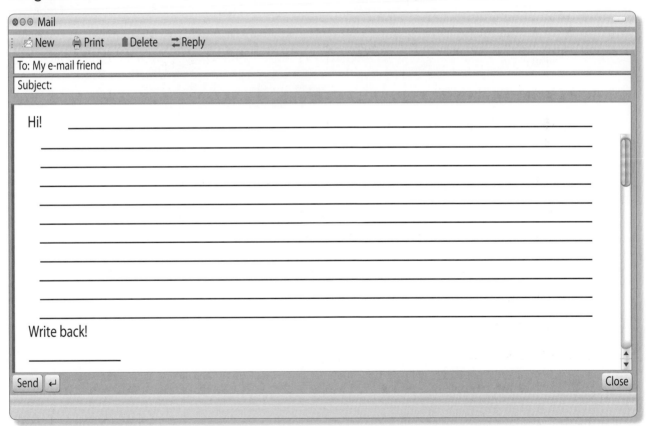

C Practice reading your e-mail with a partner at school. Take turns asking and answering questions about your timetable.

UNIT 2 What does she look like?

Vocabulary Focus

A Match each picture to the correct description.

long curly hair   short spiky hair   short straight hair   short curly hair   long straight hair

B Complete the diagram using the words in the box.

black   brown   straight   blue   curly   ~~spiky~~   short   red   long   blond   green

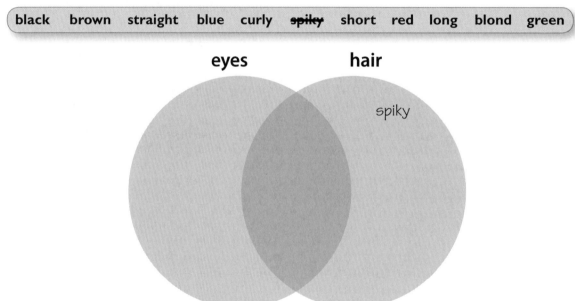

eyes   **hair**

spiky

Conversation

Complete the conversation using the words in the box. Then practice with a partner at school.

purple   eyes   hair   curly   glasses   sorry

Marcus: Hi Andy, where are you? It's 4:00!

Andy: (1) _____, Marcus. I'm still on the bus. Is my sister there yet?

Marcus: What does she look like? Does she wear (2) _____?

Andy: No, she doesn't. She has blond (3) _____ and green (4) _____.

Marcus: Does she have long (5) _____ hair?

Andy: Uh-huh. Oh yeah, she's wearing a (6) _____ T-shirt.

Marcus: There she is! Hey . . . umm . . . Andy's sister!

Language Focus

A Circle the correct words to complete the conversation. Then practice with a partner at school.

Elena: Hi, Carmen. Do you have this month's *Teen Magazine*?

Carmen: Yeah. There's a photo of my cousin Ben's band on page 30.

Elena: No way! What (*do* / *does*) they look like?

Carmen: Well . . . They (*'s* / *'re*) all boys, and they all (*has* / *have*) short spiky hair.

Elena: I found the picture. Which one is Ben? Does he (*wear* / *wears*) glasses?

Carmen: No, that's his friend, Andy. He (*'s* / *has*) medium height, right?

Elena: Uh-huh. (*Is* / *Are*) Ben short or tall? Does he (*has* / *have*) braces?

Carmen: No. He (*'s* / *'re*) quite tall and he (*has* / *have*) really red hair.

Elena: Oh! That one!

B Look at the picture of Li's family. Write the questions and answers.

1. What does Li's brother look like?

   _____

2. Does Li have short hair?

   _____

3. _____

   He's tall and wears glasses.

4. What does Li's mother look like?

   _____

C What does your family look like?

_____

_____

_____

_____

Reading

A Read the letter. Write 1 to 4 to match the description to the correct picture.

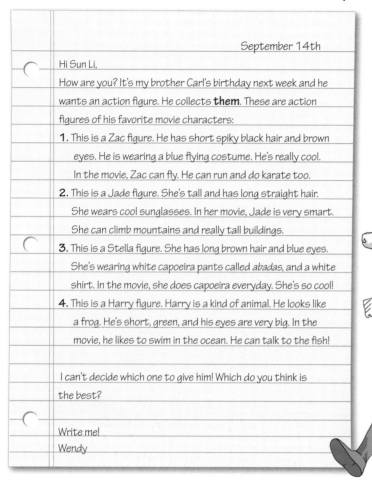

September 14th

Hi Sun Li,

How are you? It's my brother Carl's birthday next week and he wants an action figure. He collects **them**. These are action figures of his favorite movie characters:

1. This is a Zac figure. He has short spiky black hair and brown eyes. He is wearing a blue flying costume. He's really cool. In the movie, Zac can fly. He can run and do karate too.

2. This is a Jade figure. She's tall and has long straight hair. She wears cool sunglasses. In her movie, Jade is very smart. She can climb mountains and really tall buildings.

3. This is a Stella figure. She has long brown hair and blue eyes. She's wearing white capoeira pants called abadas, and a white shirt. In the movie, she does capoeira everyday. She's so cool!

4. This is a Harry figure. Harry is a kind of animal. He looks like a frog. He's short, green, and his eyes are very big. In the movie, he likes to swim in the ocean. He can talk to the fish!

I can't decide which one to give him! Which do you think is the best?

Write me!
Wendy

B Read the letter in **A** again. Answer the questions.

1. Who is Carl?
   a. Sun Li's brother   **b.** Wendy's brother   **c.** Stella's brother

2. What does the "them" in blue mean?
   a. movie actors   **b.** brothers   **c.** action figures

3. What can Jade do in the movie?
   a. fly   **b.** climb   **c.** swim

4. Who does Wendy say are cool?
   a. Zac and Harry   **b.** Stella and Harry   **c.** Zac and Stella

5. Who can do martial arts?
   a. Zac and Stella   **b.** Harry and Jade   **c.** Jade and Stella

Writing

A Draw your own action figure. What does it look like? Write a letter to a friend about it!

Hi,

This is my action figure.

My action figure

Write me ,

B Read your letter to a partner at school.
Take turns asking and answering questions.
Draw your partner's action figure.

My partner's action figure

Does he have spiky hair?

Yes, he does.

UNIT 3
How do you get to the park?

Vocabulary Focus

A Circle the 13 hidden words or phrases in blue. Words can go ← → ↑ ↓ ↖ ↗ ↙ ↘.

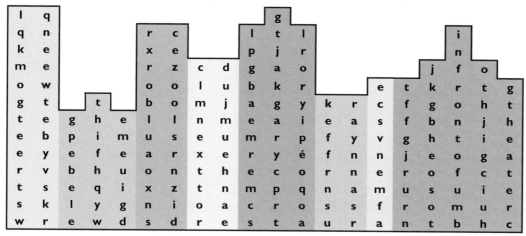

B Where is the blue house (A)? Complete the sentences using the words in the box.

in front of	behind	on the corner of	next to	between	across from

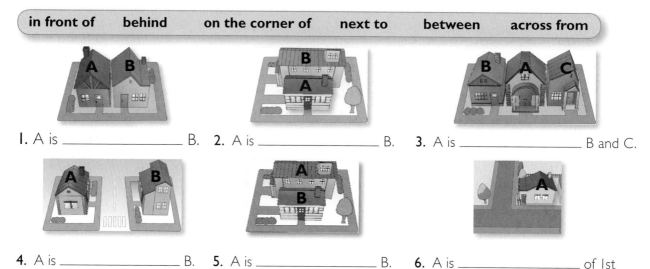

1. A is _____ B.

2. A is _____ B.

3. A is _____ B and C.

4. A is _____ B.

5. A is _____ B.

6. A is _____ of 1st and 14th Street.

Conversation

Circle the correct words to complete the conversation. Then practice with a partner at school.

Diego: Excuse me. Can you help me, please?

Kathy: Sure. Where do you want (to do / to go)?

Diego: I want to go to the museum. Is this Sixth (street / Street)?

Kathy: Yes, it is. The museum is (right / behind) across the road. Can you see it now?

Diego: Yes! OK, great. Oh, and how do I get to the night market near here?

Kathy: It's on the (corner / street) of Tenth Street and Adams Road. It's (between / in) the park. The park is (across / across from) the Grand Theater.

Diego: Oh, OK. Thanks!

Language Focus

A Correct the mistakes. Then practice with a partner at school.

Angela: Excuse ~~you~~ *me*. Can you help me?

Chris: Sure. Where do I want to go?

Angela: I want to go on the Newtown Theater, please.
How do I get there?

Chris: Go straight down this Science Road. Then turn right
in New Street. The theater is at the left.

Angela: OK, thanks you.

B Look at the map. Complete the conversations. Then practice with a partner at school.

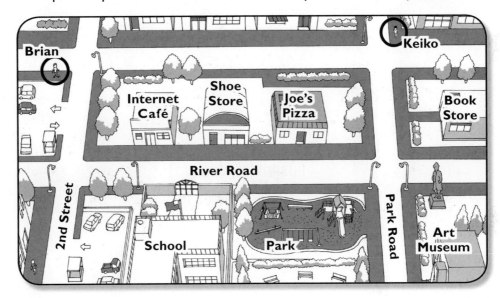

Keiko: Excuse me. How do I get to the park?

Mark: (straight) _____Go straight down Park Road._____

(past) _____

(across from) _____

Keiko: Thanks.

· ·

Brian: Excuse me. How do I get to the shoe store?

Davi: (right) _____

(left) _____

(between) _____

Brian: Thanks.

Reading

A Skim the postcard. Where is Eldora?

    a. New Jersey   **b.** New York   **c.** New Mexico

Dear Fran,

I'm in the United States now. New York City is amazing! There are a lot of things to see here, like art museums, theaters, the Bronx Zoo, and parks.

Central Park is a large park, right in the middle of the city. It's very big, Fran. It's 61 blocks long! About 25,000,000 people go there each year. The park has a zoo, a theater, and a museum. Many people walk, bike, or run there in the day.

New York has four seasons. In the summer, it is hot. A lot of people go to Central Park to swim in the lake and sit under the big trees. It's cooler there.

In the winter, it is very cold and snowy. You can't swim in the lake, but you can ice skate on it.

Well, see you when I get home next month!

Eldora

NY. NY., U.S.A.
April XX
Postal Service

To:

Fran Smith
Manzana 5 Casa 9
Puerto Escondido
Oaxaca 12345
Mexico

New York City, U.S.A.

73587

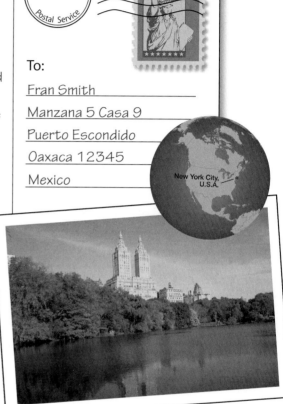

B Read the postcard in **A**. Answer the questions.

  1. Which of these does Eldora write about?

    a. schools   **b.** restaurants   **c.** theaters

  2. How many museums are there in Central Park?

    a. 1   **b.** 25   **c.** 61

  3. What's the weather like in the city in winter?

    a. It's cold and snowy.   **b.** It's cold and foggy.   **c.** It's cold and rainy.

  4. According to the postcard, what do some people do in the park?

    a. They climb.   **b.** They swim.   **c.** They ski.

  5. Where does Eldora come from?

    a. Mexico   **b.** Nevada   **c.** New York

Writing

A Look at Kara's map. Then read her report.

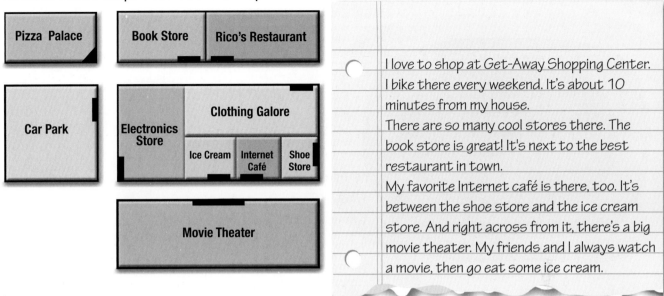

I love to shop at Get-Away Shopping Center. I bike there every weekend. It's about 10 minutes from my house.

There are so many cool stores there. The book store is great! It's next to the best restaurant in town.

My favorite Internet café is there, too. It's between the shoe store and the ice cream store. And right across from it, there's a big movie theater. My friends and I always watch a movie, then go eat some ice cream.

B Where is your favorite place to shop? Draw your own map. Then write your own report.

C Practice talking about your favorite place to shop with a partner at school. Take turns asking and answering questions.

Where do you like to shop?

I like to go to ...

Language Review 1, Units 1-3

A Circle the 11 hidden words and phrases. The words can go ← → ↑ ↓ ↖ ↗ ↙ ↘.

behind
straight
braces
freckles
medium
height
blond
natural
history
comic books
long

o	e	i	a	h	d	n	l	e	c	o
o	e	c	o	g	r	n	m	c	s	r
k	c	b	m	a	i	n	i	e	t	t
h	n	a	t	u	r	a	l	h	s	s
i	n	l	a	r	m	k	g	e	e	n
s	k	o	o	b	c	i	m	o	c	b
t	m	n	h	e	a	e	a	h	a	i
o	b	g	r	r	d	d	h	b	r	t
r	n	f	t	i	d	n	o	l	b	o
y	r	s	u	h	e	i	g	h	t	g
n	a	m	n	k	o	r	o	n	o	s

B Look at the picture. Complete the questions and answers.

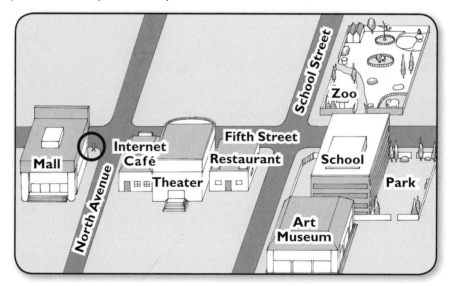

1. _____

   It's on the corner of Fifth Street and School Street, next to the park.

2. Where's the theater? _____

3. I'm looking for the zoo. _____

4. I want to go to the mall. _____

5. _____. You can see pictures there.

6. I'm at the mall. How do I get to the art museum?

   _____

   _____

   _____

   _____

C Fill in the blanks to complete James's message.

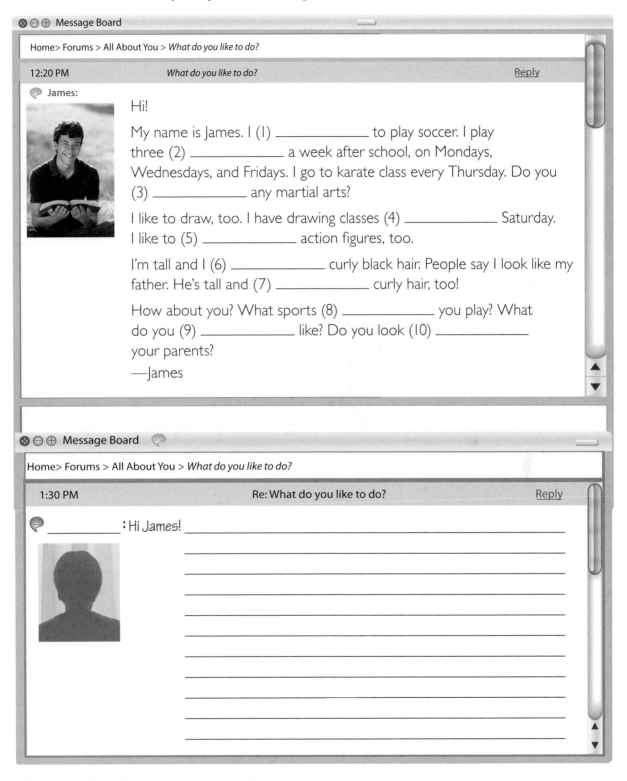

Message Board

Home> Forums > All About You > *What do you like to do?*

| 12:20 PM | *What do you like to do?* | Reply |

James:

Hi!

My name is James. I (1) _____ to play soccer. I play three (2) _____ a week after school, on Mondays, Wednesdays, and Fridays. I go to karate class every Thursday. Do you (3) _____ any martial arts?

I like to draw, too. I have drawing classes (4) _____ Saturday. I like to (5) _____ action figures, too.

I'm tall and I (6) _____ curly black hair. People say I look like my father. He's tall and (7) _____ curly hair, too!

How about you? What sports (8) _____ you play? What do you (9) _____ like? Do you look (10) _____ your parents?
—James

Message Board

Home> Forums > All About You > *What do you like to do?*

| 1:30 PM | Re: What do you like to do? | Reply |

_____ : Hi James! _____

_____

_____

_____

_____

_____

_____

_____

_____

_____

_____

D Write a reply to James's message in **C**.

E Read your message with a partner at school. Then take turns asking and answering questions about your messages.

What's the coldest place on Earth?

Vocabulary Focus

Look at the picture. Circle the 11 hidden words.

Conversation

Complete the conversation using the words in the box. Then practice with a partner at school.

| the tallest | the longest | Desert | the highest | tomorrow |
| the lowest | the hottest | minute | the largest | Sea |

Risa: Hi, Lee! What are you studying?

Lee: Geography. I've got a test (1) _____. Did you know that Mount Everest is
        (2) _____ mountain in the world? It's over 8,848 meters (29,029 feet) high.

Risa: Really? That's cool. So, what's (3) _____ place on Earth?

Lee: It's the Dead (4) _____. It's 422 meters (1,385 feet) below sea level.

Risa: Do you know what's (5) _____ waterfall in the world?

Lee: No, I don't. Do you know?

Risa: Uh-huh. It's Angel Falls. How about (6) _____ river?

Lee: I know that one! That's the Nile. And (7) _____ river is the Amazon River.
        Hey Risa, where's the Sahara (8) _____?

Risa: Um . . . just a (9) _____ . . . I think it's in Africa.

Lee: Oh, OK! My teacher says it's (10) _____ place on Earth.

Language Focus

A Match the questions with the correct answers.

The Vatican City

Paris

Yuma

Tokyo

Ireland

1. Is it rainy in Ireland? •   • **a.** No, it's the most expensive city on Earth.

2. Is living in Tokyo cheap? •   • **b.** Yes, it is. It's the sunniest place on Earth.

3. Is the food in Paris good? •   • **c.** No, it's the smallest country in the world!

4. Is it sunny in Yuma, Arizona? •   • **d.** Yes. My aunt says it's the best in the world.

5. Is the Vatican City big? •   • **e.** Yes, it's one of the rainiest places in Europe!

B Read the answers. Then write the questions.

1. _Where does the smallest dog in the world live?_ _____

    The smallest dog in the world lives in the United States.

2. _____

    The largest animal on Earth is the blue whale. They can grow up to 32 meters (105 feet) long and weigh 200 tons.

3. _____

    The tallest person in the world is Sultan Kösen, from Turkey.

4. _____

    The most expensive guitar in the world costs US$2,700,000.

5. _____

    The wettest place in Asia is in India.

C Answer the questions.

1. Who's the tallest student in your class? _____

2. Who's the best soccer player in your school? _____

3. What's the biggest store in your neighborhood? _____

Reading

A Look at the title and picture. What is this article about?

    a. text messages

    b. studying English

    c. money

The Fastest Fingers in the United States

This is 15-year-old Kate Moore from Des Moines, Iowa, in the United States. Kate loves to text. She usually writes 400–470 text messages a day. That's over 14,000 text messages a month! She studies with her friends by texting, and she looks at the text messages just before her tests.

In this picture, Kate is in New York. Does she want to see the most famous person in America or the tallest building in New York City? No. She wants to see if she can be the best texter in the United States. She is here for the biggest texting competition in the country. Over 250,000 people want to be in this competition, and they all think they are the best at texting.

Guess what? Kate is the fastest in the United States! She gets a $50,000 prize! Kate has a message for parents who do not like it when their children text. She tells them to let their sons and daughters text. Maybe they can win $50,000, too!

B Read the article in **A**. Circle **T** (true) or **F** (false).

    1. **T** **(F)**   Kate is 14 years old.

    2. **T** **F**   Kate sends 400 text messages a month.

    3. **T** **F**   Kate uses her cell phone to study.

    4. **T** **F**   Kate is from New York.

    5. **T** **F**   Kate is the fastest texter in the United States.

    6. **T** **F**   Kate thinks it is okay to let children text.

C Correct the false sentences.

    1. Kate is 15 years old.

    _____

    _____

    _____

Writing

A Complete the chart with information about your friends and family.

Who has/is . . .		
the longest hair	**the best at sports**	**the most interesting hobby**
the tallest	**the quietest**	**your idea:**

B Using the information in **A**, write a letter to a friend about your friends and family.

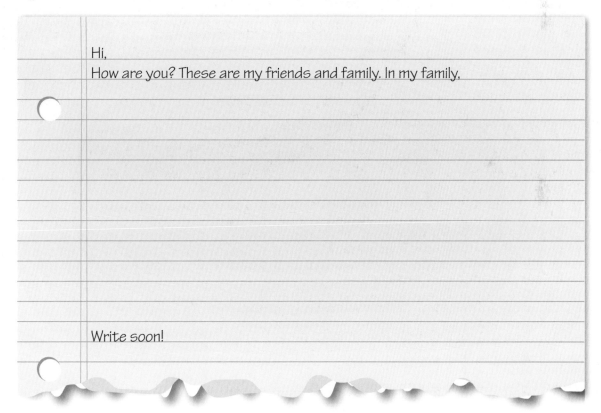

Hi,
How are you? These are my friends and family. In my family,

Write soon!

C Practice reading your letter with a partner at school. Then take turns asking and answering questions.

In my family, my father is the tallest. Who's the tallest in your family, Ming?

Actually ... uh ... I am!

Are cats cuter than dogs?

Vocabulary Focus

A Look at the pictures. Write a check (✓) in the correct box for each description.

1. more playful

2. cleaner

3. more dangerous

4. gentler

B What word is different? Circle it.

1. cat	hippo	rabbit	bird
2. more playful	more intelligent	more independent	more dangerous
3. nicer	cuter	scarier	gentler
4. cuter	tiger	friendlier	better
5. rhino	elephant	leopard	rabbit

Conversation

Complete the conversation using the words in the box. Then practice with a partner at school.

> friendlier   more   leopards   which   more intelligent

Juliana: Hey Tomas, today on *The Amazing Race*, the last two teams go to Africa!

Tomas: Hi Juliana! I know, it's (1) _____ dangerous than before.

Juliana: They see elephants, rhinos, and (2) _____.

Tomas: (3) _____ team do you think is better?

Juliana: I think Team B is better. They speak a lot of languages. They're
(4) _____ than Team C.

Tomas: Maybe, but I still like Team C better. They're always helping other teams.
They're (5) _____ than Team B.

Language Focus

A Circle the correct words to complete the conversations. Then practice with a partner at school.

Sara: Who do you think is
(famous / more famous),
Jesse McCartney or Zac Efron?

Belle: I think Jesse is. He's a
(good / better) singer than Zac.

Sara: Really? I disagree. Zac is
(cuter / more cute) than Jesse.

Belle: Well, that's true. But Jesse looks
(more intelligent / intelligenter)
than Zac.

Sam: Wow! Look, Tom! This baby lion is
(as small as / smaller) a cat.

Josh: Cool! Do you think the baby lion looks
more (playful than / playful) a cat?

Sam: Uh, I think the baby lion is as playful
(than / as) a cat. Lions and cats are
from the same family, you know.

Josh: But a cat isn't as
(dangerous / more dangerous)
as a lion.

B Look at the chart. Write the questions and answers.

		Height	Weight	Life	Deepest Dive
	Emperor Penguin	About 115 cm	Up to 40 kg	15–20 years	534 m (1,752 feet)
Adélie Penguin		About 70 cm	4 to 5.5 kg	20 years	176 m (577 feet)

1. Which penguin is taller?

   _____

2. Which penguin lives longer?

   _____

3. Which penguin can dive deeper?

   _____

4. _____

   An emperor penguin is heavier than an Adélie penguin.

C Answer the questions.

1. Which do you think is cuter, emperor or Adélie penguins? _____

2. Which subject do you like better, math or science? _____

Reading

A Look at the report. What is it about?

  a. Sam's trip to Antarctica

  b. people in Antarctica

  c. animals in Antarctica

Welcome to Antarctica!

Antarctica is colder, drier, and windier than the other continents on Earth. 98% of the land in Antarctica is ice. In Antarctica, winter starts in March. And winter there is worse than in other countries. It is too cold for a lot of animals, so many of the animals leave during the winter. But emperor penguins don't leave.

Emperor penguins are larger than other penguins. Which do you think are bigger, male or female emperor penguins? Actually, neither are bigger. Male penguins are as tall and as big as females.

Emperor penguins are very intelligent. In winter, they stand in a

big group to keep warm. The inside of the group is warmer than the outside, so all the penguins take turns. Sometimes they are on the inside, and sometimes they are on the outside of the group, so they never get too cold.

There are many different animals and fish in Antarctica. One group of animals is called sea cucumbers. They live in the sea. Some of these animals look like

worms, but they are a lot bigger than worms. Some sea cucumbers are very long. Some are as long as an emperor penguin!

Antarctica has many kinds of amazing animals. I want to go there and see them all.

by Sam Fisher   June 22

B Read the report in **A**. Circle the correct letter to complete each sentence.

1. According to Sam's report, Antarctica is the _____ continent on Earth.

   a. coldest, driest, and windiest   b. nicest, coolest, and best   c. scariest, darkest, and snowiest

2. Female emperor penguins are _____ than male emperor penguins.

   a. bigger   b. smaller   c. as big as

3. The inside of the group of emperor penguins is _____ the outside.

   a. warmer than   b. colder than   c. as cool as

4. According to Sam's report, some _____ are as long as emperor penguins.

   a. worms   b. sea cucumbers   c. fish

5. Sam _____.

   a. lives in Antarctica   b. is visiting Antarctica   c. wants to go to Antarctica

Writing

A Complete the word web with information about your town or a city you know.

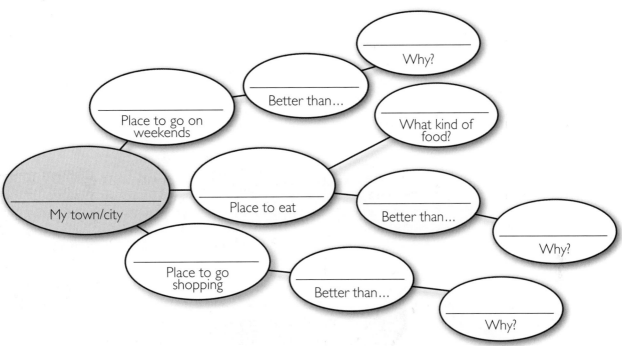

B Read Kenji's letter. Then using the information in **A**, write a reply to him.

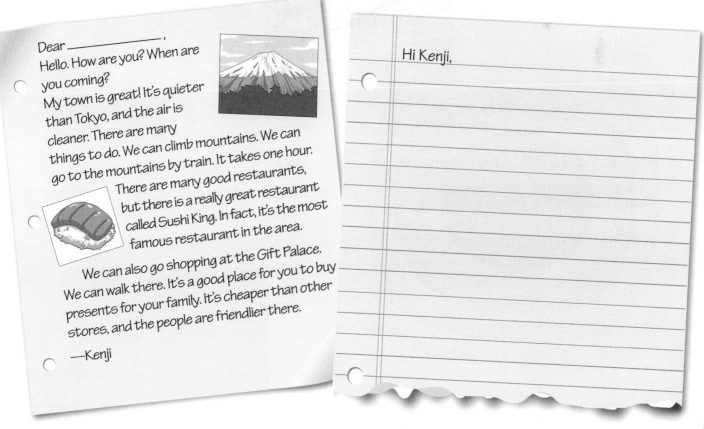

Dear _____,
Hello. How are you? When are you coming?
My town is great! It's quieter than Tokyo, and the air is cleaner. There are many things to do. We can climb mountains. We can go to the mountains by train. It takes one hour.
There are many good restaurants, but there is a really great restaurant called Sushi King. In fact, it's the most famous restaurant in the area.
We can also go shopping at the Gift Palace. We can walk there. It's a good place for you to buy presents for your family. It's cheaper than other stores, and the people are friendlier there.

—Kenji

Hi Kenji,

C Practice reading your letter with a partner at school.

How was your trip?

Vocabulary Focus

What did the *Time Zones* team do? Look at the picture and complete the sentences.

> went hiking   went to the beach   saw many animals   swam in the ocean   ate interesting food

The *Time Zones* team took a trip.

They all _____.

Ming _____.

Nadine _____.

Stig _____.

Maya _____.

Conversation

Put the conversation in the correct order from 1 to 6. Then practice with a partner at school.

a. _____ Yeah, they were really amazing.

b. __1__ Hi, Ethan. How was your trip to China? Where did you go?

c. _____ Wow! Xi'an! What did you do there?

d. _____ Yum! Did you see the terracotta soldiers there?

e. _____ Hi, Ming. I went to Xi'an. It was really great! I had so much fun.

f. _____ I walked on the city wall. And I ate lots of interesting food.

Language Focus

A Circle the correct words to complete the conversation. Then practice with a partner at school.

Mother: Hi, Daisuke. So, where (*are* / *were*) you now?

Daisuke: Hi, Mom! I'm in Peru. Yesterday, we (*took* / *take*) a bus for 10 hours!

Mother: Really? Did you (*see* / *saw*) any interesting things?

Daisuke: Yeah, Mom, I saw so many interesting things! I (*see* / *saw*) the Amazon River. It was so big!

Mother: That's wonderful, Daisuke. Did you (*swim* / *swam*) in the river?

Daisuke: No, but we (*visit* / *visited*) an amazing museum.

Mother: Where (*do* / *did*) you stay last night?

Daisuke: We (*stayed* / *stay*) at a hotel in the city. I'm there now.

B Look at the picture of Olivia. Complete the sentences.

When Olivia was 5 years old, . . .

1. (play soccer)   she played soccer.

2. (play the piano)

3. (eat hamburgers)

4. (have long hair)

5. (like dresses)

5 YEARS OLD

Reading

A Look at the website. Who are the people in the picture?

    a. An American student staying with a family in Thailand.

    b. A Chinese student staying with a family in Brazil.

    c. A Brazilian student staying with a family in the United States.

STUDY THE ENGLISH LANGUAGE United States

username

password

LOGIN

Home   About   Levels   Classes   Specials   Order

Join

"You can have fun studying English, too!"

I love speaking English, so I went to an English language school in the United States. My class was quite small. There was one student from China, two from Thailand, one from Sweden, and me. At the language school, we studied English every morning, Monday through Friday. In the afternoon, we visited famous places.

I lived with an American family. My American "father" is a teacher, and my "mother" is a teacher, too. They have two sons and one daughter. We played outside on the weekends. I had so much fun!

It was winter in Brazil, but it was summer in the U.S. It was so hot! One day, it was 40 degrees! Most days it wasn't too hot. You can have fun learning English, too! Go to the United States for a month and study English, like I did!

— Yara

B Read the text in **A**. Answer the questions.

1. How many students were in her class?
    a. four   b. five   c. six

2. What did Yara do in the morning on weekdays?
    a. She played outside.   b. She visited many places.   c. She studied English.

3. What did Yara do on weekday afternoons?
    a. She studied at the school.   b. She visited famous places.   c. She played sports outside.

4. When did Yara play outside?
    a. on Saturdays and Sundays   b. on Tuesdays and Wednesdays   c. on Mondays and Fridays

5. How long was Yara in the United States?
    a. about a week   b. about 30 days   c. about two months

Writing

A Think about a trip you made, or pretend that you took a trip. Complete the chat.

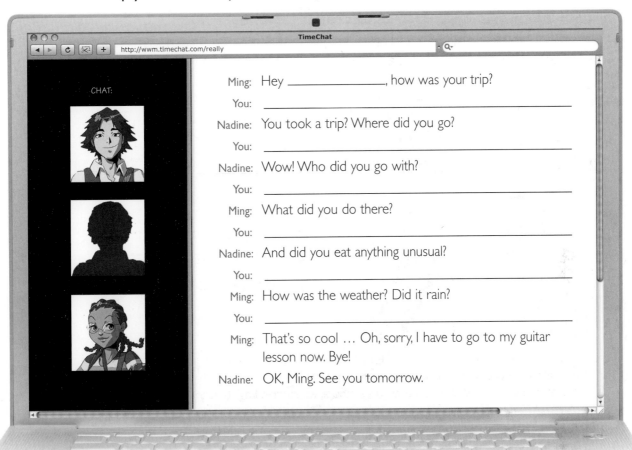

TimeChat

http://wwm.timechat.com/really

CHAT:

Ming: Hey _____, how was your trip?

You: _____

Nadine: You took a trip? Where did you go?

You: _____

Nadine: Wow! Who did you go with?

You: _____

Ming: What did you do there?

You: _____

Nadine: And did you eat anything unusual?

You: _____

Ming: How was the weather? Did it rain?

You: _____

Ming: That's so cool … Oh, sorry, I have to go to my guitar lesson now. Bye!

Nadine: OK, Ming. See you tomorrow.

B Using the information in **A**, write a report about your trip.

_____

_____

_____

_____

_____

C Practice reading your report with a partner at school. Then, take turns asking and answering questions about your trip.

Language Review 2, Units 4–6

A Look at the words in the box. Then use them to complete the puzzle.

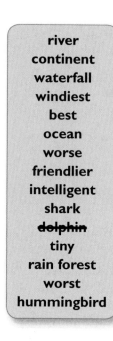

river
continent
waterfall
windiest
best
ocean
worse
friendlier
intelligent
shark
~~dolphin~~
tiny
rain forest
worst
hummingbird

B Read the answers. Then write the questions.

1. _____
   No, dolphins are more intelligent than sharks.

2. _____
   Cats are more popular than dogs.

3. _____
   Cats are more independent than dogs.

4. _____
   A whale is the largest animal in the world.

C Match the questions with the correct answers.

1. Is Mark at school today? •

2. Jane, did you do your homework? •

3. Do you study Spanish? •

4. Where did you go for your vacation? •

5. Did you see that bird? •

6. Who did you dance with? •

• a. Yes, and I studied it last year too.

• b. I danced with my friend, Wally.

• c. Yeah, I saw it! It was really pretty.

• d. I went to South Africa.

• e. I did it this morning, Mom.

• f. He was there this morning, but he's not there now.

D Look at the pictures. Then fill in the blanks to complete the text.

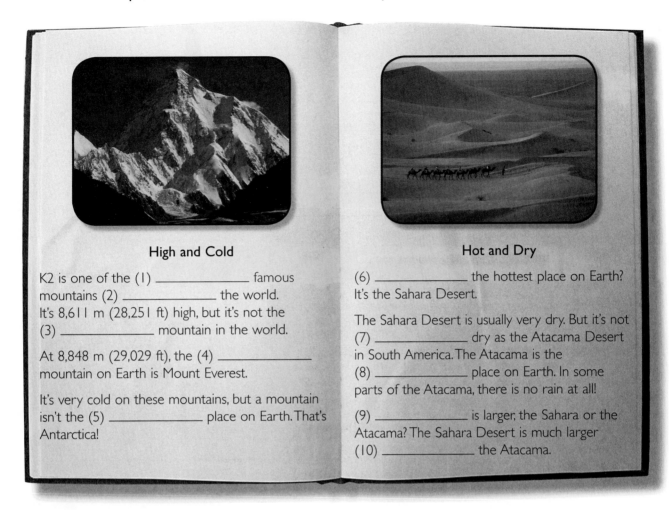

High and Cold

K2 is one of the (1) _____ famous mountains (2) _____ the world. It's 8,611 m (28,251 ft) high, but it's not the (3) _____ mountain in the world.

At 8,848 m (29,029 ft), the (4) _____ mountain on Earth is Mount Everest.

It's very cold on these mountains, but a mountain isn't the (5) _____ place on Earth. That's Antarctica!

Hot and Dry

(6) _____ the hottest place on Earth? It's the Sahara Desert.

The Sahara Desert is usually very dry. But it's not (7) _____ dry as the Atacama Desert in South America. The Atacama is the (8) _____ place on Earth. In some parts of the Atacama, there is no rain at all!

(9) _____ is larger, the Sahara or the Atacama? The Sahara Desert is much larger (10) _____ the Atacama.

E Answer the questions.

1. What did you do last weekend? _____
2. Did you watch TV last night? What did you watch? _____
3. How was your last vacation? _____
4. What music did you listen to last week? _____
5. Which is more fun, math or science? _____
6. Which do you like more, summer vacation or winter vacation? _____

F Read the questions and your answers in **E** with a partner at school.
Take turns asking and answering.

Did you watch TV last night?

What did you watch?

Yes, I did!

I watched . . .

The Real World Quiz 1, Units 1–3

A How do you get to school? Label the pictures.

 I take the bus.

 _____

 _____  _____

 _____

B Complete the text using the words in the box.

sport	best	players	jump	famous	ski	position

I can water (1) _____, but I can't do the high
(2) _____. My favorite team (3) _____ is ice
hockey. In ice hockey, there are six (4) _____ on a team.
Stefan Liv is my favorite player. His (5) _____ is goaltender.
What's your favorite sport? Who's the (6) _____ player
on your favorite team? Is that person (7) _____?

C What are they feeling? Label the pictures.

1.  _____

2. _____

3. _____

4.  _____

5.  _____

D Unscramble the idioms.

1. up / drives / me / the / wall / he _____
2. face / a / straight / keep _____
3. has / two / feet / he / left _____

The Real World Quiz 2, Units 4–6

A Match the questions with the correct answers.

1. Which city has the most people living inside it?   •

2. How many people live in Europe?   •

3. What's the biggest city in area?   •

4. Which continent has the most people?   •

• **a.** 731 million people live there.

• **b.** Mumbai, India. It has fourteen million people.

• **c.** Asia. There are four billion people there.

• **d.** Altamira, Brazil. It's about 1,800 times bigger than Manhattan, New York.

B What are these animals saying? You can use the words in the box below, or write your own ideas.

afraid	alert	angry	comfortable
curious	excited	playful	sad

C Write 1 to 6 to put the mountain summits in order from highest to the lowest.

KILIMANJARO   MCKINLEY   ELBRUS   EVEREST   ACONCAGUA   VINSON

____   ____   ____   ____   ____   ____

D Draw lines to complete each short conversation. Then practice with a partner at school.

1. Let's go play basketball.   •

2. What is she saying?   •

3. Today is the class picnic.   •

• **a.** I don't know. She talks a mile a minute!

• **b.** Sorry. I can't. I have a mountain of work.

• **c.** Oh no! Look. It's starting to rain cats and dogs. Let's have lunch inside today.

Credits

PHOTO CREDITS